ADAPT

Copyright

Edited by Gillian Ryan Katsoulis

Published by Jarrod Davis

First Edition – 2016

ADAPT

Building Strong
Meaningful Relationships
Through Self Discovery

Jarrod Davis

Dedication

First and foremost, I want to apologize to all those people that I may have offended, insulted, degraded, and demeaned throughout my life. If I made you feel anything less than valued, if I did not lift you up and support you how I should have, I am sorry. Thanks for all that you taught me.

This book is dedicated to people who may feel as if they are misunderstood. It is also to those of you who need to learn to understand. To any person that may want to lead and find themselves alone, or a boss that has problems relating to his employees, please be open to learning.

It's dedicated to a wife or a husband who needs to make a change. It's dedicated to a Dad or Mom who needs to strengthen their relationship with their children. It's dedicated to a friend, a family, a co-worker, and even to a stranger you may pass in the street.

Most importantly, it's dedicated to my family, all of whom I love very much. May I always follow my own message, not only for me but for you as well!

Access your DISC personality assessment for **FREE** at
<u>adaptthebook.com</u>

Table of Contents

"When I was a young man, I wanted to change the world. I found it was difficult to change the world, so I tried to change my nation.

When I found I couldn't change the nation, I began to focus on my town. I couldn't change the town and as an older man, I tried to change my family.

Now, as an old man, I realize the only thing I can change is myself, and suddenly I realize that if long ago I had changed myself, I could have made an impact on my family. My family and I could have made an impact on our town. Their impact could have changed the nation and I could indeed have changed the world."

–Unknown Monk (ca.1100 AD)

Introduction

Nobody succeeds alone...EVER! So, what if you were able to hand pick exactly who you had to work with and be around everyday? What if you had the ability to get people to do what you expected them to do all the time? What if you could get everyone around to support you in reaching the pinnacle of success? That would be great, but the reality is that in most areas of life you don't get to choose who you are around. What you can do however, is learn to build relationships with the people around you so they want to do what you expect and support you in your success.

For the most part, you don't get to choose who's on your team, who your co-workers are, and in many cases who your boss is. If you are to succeed in life, you need to recognize that your level of success, satisfaction, and happiness will often depend on your ability to get along with people.

Unless you're a hermit living off the land in a desolate forest, you are surrounded by people every day. You may be married with kids or have brothers and sisters. I don't know your particular situation, but I do know that you have people in your life in some form or fashion.

There are people who take your order at the drive through, people who scan your groceries at the cash register, and people on the other end of the phone when you call a customer service number. You pass them in the halls at work, you answer to them in the office, and you help them with their projects. They are your co-workers, your friends, and your customers.

The point is that if you're surrounded by them for most of your day, wouldn't it make sense to learn how to maximize your level of success in building relationships with them?

Like I said, nobody succeeds alone. So in order to live a life of fulfillment, you have to recognize the impact as well as the importance of relationships and the roles they play in your life. Then learn to adapt who you are and who you are being with those you surround yourself with. They will ultimately hold control over how far you get in life and, I assume, your goal is to get as far as possible.

Learning who *you* are and identifying the roadblocks that are keeping you from establishing strong relationships is the first step. Then, you'll need to learn how to recognize who others are and how you can best relate to them. In doing this, you can quickly build stronger, more successful relationships.

In life you ultimately get to make choices for one person and that person is *you*. As much as you might like to control other people, their choices, and their behavior, you can't. By taking responsibility for your actions and learning to lead people how they want to be led, you will accomplish your goals and allow others to take action in a way that makes them comfortable.

Once you have established who you are and the role others play in your life, you need to take steps toward building stronger relationships with them.

By recognizing how people communicate best, learning to give feedback in a receptive way, understanding that growth may be uncomfortable, and adopting a mindset that everybody has value, you are well on your way to creating relationships that will support you in living a happy and fulfilled life.

Your level of success in life depends on you taking responsibility for your actions and learning how to connect with people. The key to this book is to give you the tools to recognize where you need to make changes, develop the skills required to make these changes happen, and adopt the attitude that will guide you toward success.

We have to understand that it isn't *what happens* to us that affects our behavior but rather *our interpretation of what happens* to us. If you can change how you think about your interactions with others, you are on a path to significant change and more effective habits.

By adopting the ideas in this book, you can make your entire family stronger, your interactions with strangers more rewarding, and your relationships with co-workers better. That can lead to a happier and more productive work and home environment.

Today is the day that you begin to live a life on purpose. Today is the day you start living a happier, purpose-driven, and more fulfilling life.

The Story

As the sun shone through the window in John's bedroom he rolled over from a deep sleep and glanced at the clock. John suddenly sprang to his feet in surprise. "Who turned off my alarm!?!" he yelled at his wife, Sarah, sleeping next to him. "It's 7:23 and now I'm going to be late!!"

He jumped out of bed and ran to his closet to get his clothes for the day. "Where is my white shirt?" he shouted at his wife who was still trying to wake up. "I assume it's still in the laundry, you wore it a few days ago," she replied. "You know I wear that shirt on days I have meetings. This is my meeting day and I can't believe that you didn't have it cleaned for me. What am I going to wear now?" His wife, Sarah, scrambled to her feet to help John find something to wear to his meeting. "Sorry John I didn't know you had a meeting this morning. I wish you had told me. I would have washed it for you."

Sarah found John a shirt in the back of the closet and quickly ironed it for him. John put on a pair of pants he pulled out of the closet, grabbed the shirt without even a thank you and put it on. "I need your help tying my tie. And don't make it too short!" he yelled.

After getting dressed, he rushed out the door to head to the office without kissing his wife or even saying goodbye. He jumped in the car, started the engine, and backed out of the driveway. As he put the car in drive he noticed that he only had a 1/8 of a tank of gas. He muttered under his breath, "Just my luck. Running late and of course I have to be out of gas! I am sick and tired of always rushing. If traffic hadn't been so bad last night I could have gotten it then!"

As he pulled into the gas station, there was a lineup at the gas pumps. He noticed one pump was occupied as a woman chatted to the guy behind her. She was laughing and it was obvious they were just making small talk. John rolled down his window and yelled to the lady, "I'm late for work and I need to get gas. If you don't mind having your morning social somewhere other than at the pumps it would be greatly appreciated!" The lady looked at John and, obviously annoyed by his comment, yelled back, "Bad planning on your part doesn't give you the right to treat people like dirt!" She got in her car and pulled away from the pump.

It was no big deal to John and frankly the lady should have realized her stupidity as the pumps are no place to have silly conversations. He quickly filled up his car and off he went to the office.

John pulled into the parking lot and gathered his things from the front seat. He was late and completely focused on getting to his meeting. He walked through the front door and past his administrative assistant, Amy, without even as much as a good morning. He headed straight into his office, closing the door behind him.

Before too long John came rushing out of his office muttering under his breath, "Well this is going to be a complete flop! I'm not even a bit prepared for this!" As he walked into the meeting, he noticed that everybody was already there waiting for him. "Sorry I'm late, my wife didn't set my alarm this morning, the laundry wasn't done, and of course there was no gas in the car. I'm not as prepared for this meeting as I should be. Amy didn't get a chance to send me the numbers sooner and I had to get everything ready myself."

John's administrative assistant sat at the opposite end of the table a little bit confused as she was more than willing to help John get prepared, he just never asked her. As she sat there thinking to herself she began to reflect on how John ignored her this morning. Maybe he had purposefully not asked for her help. She started to worry, knowing now that he wasn't happy with her. Was she about to get fired? She realized that John didn't appreciate her and she always felt like she needed to walk on egg shells when he was around. She thought about how unhappy she was working for John and that maybe she should start looking for a new job anyway.

At work, and at home, John wasn't building very many positive relationships. In fact, it was quite the opposite. People were actually afraid of John and avoided him as much as possible. His behavior alienated him from others, so he found himself doing all the work in order to get anything done. Was it really other people's fault or was John creating much of his own frustration?

If John changed his behavior and learned to respect the people around him, could he possibly get more help and support? Could John get more work done and even make more money with other people helping him? Could John live a much happier and fulfilling life by changing his own behavior and take responsibility for his actions?

What about Sarah and Amy? If they recognized why John's behavior made them feel the way it does, could that make it any better? Whether it's right or wrong, could they do something that might benefit them and also help John see how he was affecting them?

In many ways, I have been John throughout my life. I think, though, you might see yourself in John as well. At different points in life, we all play the role of John, Sarah, or Amy. But we don't have to react like any of them. We can take responsibility for our own situations and make changes that will guide us toward happier and more effective relationships.

The truth is that the quicker we take responsibility for our behavior and recognize how to adapt to other people, the faster we will be able to climb the ladder of success, whether in marriage, family, or at the office as an employee or manager. Whether you are someone who runs over others, or someone who gets run over, you don't have to let that hold you back in life. Recognize the opportunity that hides within every situation and take control of where you are going.

I don't claim to be the greatest leader, but I do strive to always put other people first. To have genuine conversations with people and to help point them in the right direction so that they can live purposeful and meaningful lives.

What I share with you in this book is something that most of us take for granted. Although the principles are simple, the actions required may not be. Adapting is about taking action in order to get better results with people and I think it is the missing link to our success in life. When people want to be successful leaders they miss the most important piece: the work and purposeful action it takes to connect with people. John Maxwell[1] puts it like this: "People do not care how much you know until they know how much you care."

This quote could not be more true. In our quest for leadership, this the first step in growing ourselves. For years I focused on *me* becoming what I envisioned rather than becoming what others needed me to be. I looked at it from the perspective of what I could do, rather than what we could do together as a team. The truth is, though, that no one person has ever accomplished much on their own, but together they have changed the world.

"Relationships are the foundation of Life, and Communication is the foundation of Relationships."

–Robert A. Rohm, Ph.D.

Chapter 1

What's the Secret?

What is the value you put on the ability to build great relationships with people? How do you really think it affects your outcome in life and your level of happiness? Your ability to succeed at work? In your marriage? In your relationships with your children? If you could put a price tag on an ability to build better relationships, how much would you be willing to pay?

I would guess that most people wouldn't pay for it at all. Most people don't place any value in their ability to build relationships with those around them. And that is part of the problem. Building relationships with others is, without a doubt, one of the greatest abilities and opportunities you will ever have. It will ultimately guide your success and help you live a happy and fulfilled life.

This is one area that is often taken for granted. Day in and day out, we just let relationships happen as if they weren't integral to our success and happiness. For some of us this is not a big problem. Many people have a natural skill for building relationships. For others, however, poor relationships create daily roadblocks in all areas of life.

If you ask some of the greatest leaders, teachers, business owners, and psychologists what the difference is between those who succeed or those who don't, they will tell you that the ones with people skills are more likely to be successful. Paul J. Meyer is recognized as one of the world's most outstanding authorities in the field of personal and professional development. He says, "Communication—the human connection—is the key to personal and career success." It really doesn't matter where you are, what you want to do, or with whom you want to do it: if you can win with people, you most definitely have the key to winning in life.

The major obstacle we, as people, have to overcome is that we take relationships for granted. Our ability to build and keep healthy relationships is the most important factor to reaching our potential in every aspect of life. By taking relationships for granted, we tend not to actively and continuously put effort into being aware of how we react, and ultimately how others respond to us in our daily lives.

If others respond well, you are more likely to have a higher rate of success and achievement. If others respond negatively, you are more likely to face roadblocks you'll need to overcome. Your job in every interaction is to be aware of potential obstacles and to find solutions to avoid them.

I am sure that you have been on a team, either at work or at home, with someone who didn't agree with the rest of the team. This person probably did everything they could to put up roadblocks to the team's success. In situations like these, you have two choices: to remove that person from the team, or to get that person on board with your vision.

Ask yourself how much more effective the team could have been if that person had been engaged from the beginning. What caused this person to become disengaged, and who was responsible?

Consider how different your life would be if everybody involved was positively engaged. How much more effective could you be? What role do you play in making that happen?

Lead the Way

I often think about what it takes to be a great leader and why this world is in desperate need of great leadership. Inherent leadership ability is not the most important ingredient. But then what is? What does every leader need to be great? The answer: followers. As John Maxwell,[2] one of my mentors, says, "He who thinks he leads, but has no followers, is only taking a walk."

What we know to be true is that the more followers a leader has, the more opportunity they have to influence people, which in turn helps them reach the pinnacle of success.

I worked for an organization for many years where they preached that the key to success was in finding great leaders to run companies. Working within that organization, I found they were very often shorthanded in terms of these great leaders. There never seemed to be enough of them. In a world that seeks leadership, we need more people to develop key leadership skills to lead us into the future.

In my experience, I have found that it is often the ability to build meaningful relationships that is missing from those who strive to be leaders. While many have a great vision and the confidence to stand up in a crowd of people, they lack an ability to build lasting bonds and a loyal followership. As individuals and leaders, you need to build relationships to get buy-in from the people around you. So, if you can focus on developing stronger meaningful relationships, you can improve your leadership skills and become a better leader.

This book is not specifically about becoming a great leader or developing effective leadership skills. Rather, it is about adapting your behavior and building relationships with the people around you. These concepts will help you build a foundation of effective leadership principles, especially when it comes to developing strong relationships. By embodying the concepts in this book, you will find that you begin to gain followers, establish meaningful relationships, and naturally, you become a great leader not only with your co-workers or employees but also with people that you are close with on a personal level.

As in everything, I truly believe your mindset and how you see things plays a huge role in your success. We think of leaders as powerful, innovative, successful, and assertive. Although those are all great attributes of a leader, we often miss one of the most important things: the greatest leaders *grew* to be great, they were not just born with it.

We often want to make leadership more complicated than it is. Leadership is about influence, and influence is about communicating with people so that they want to follow you. So, instead of asking yourself how you can be a better leader, you need to begin with this simple idea: how do you get people to want to follow you?

The ability to adapt and connect with others can drastically change the number of people that will follow you. This is one of the most important aspects of growing into a great leader: learning to adapt to those around you. You need to relate to people in a way that makes them want to listen to what you have to say.

But this book is not just about leadership and building your followership, it is about making yourself happier, creating more opportunity for success, and bettering your interactions with those around you.

If you look at how much time the average person spends interacting with others in their lifetime, you will understand the true value in grasping these principles and applying them daily. The average person will spend over 460,000 hours awake, and over 90,000 of those hours at work. The remainder of that time will likely be spent with friends, family, and spouses. For 460,000 hours of your life, it may be worth your time to figure out how to build relationships, for your sake, and for those around you.

So, what does adapt mean? To adapt is "to change your behavior so that it is easier to live in a particular place or situation."[3] So by definition, adapting is adjusting and modifying your current condition into one that may be more suitable for the environment you're in. However, for some reason we have been programmed to expect others to make those adjustments rather than make them ourselves.

When you think about it from that perspective does it change your way of thinking? Now you stop thinking about yourself and what *others can do for you*, and start thinking about others and *what you can do for them*. This is the master key to success with people.

The principles in this book can be applied to all aspects of life. Embodying these ideas will not only improve your ability to lead, but it will strengthen your marriage and your relationships with your children, and lead to a happier and more productive work environment.

Success through People

When you look to the top leaders in the world today, the one thing that seems to be the common thread is that none of them did it alone. That simply means they had to work with and grow through other people, ultimately mastering the skill of how to build strong, trusting relationships with the people around them.

If you look at some of our childhood fictional characters like Batman, he had Robin and Sherlock Holmes had Doctor Watson. They may only be characters, but even in our own creative minds we recognize that people who accomplish great things depend on others to be successful in their individual missions.

Bill Gates founded Microsoft in 1975 with co-founder Paul Allen. Gates would not have found as much success without him. Paul Allen, respectively, is among the 60 richest people in the world, yet most people don't even know his name.

When Apple was founded in 1976, Steve Jobs was not the only mastermind. Apple was co-founded with his partners Steve Wozniak and Ronald Wayne. They would likely not exist today if it hadn't been for them all working together. Jobs wouldn't have had the success and notoriety he had without them.

In 1999 Michael Jordan was named the greatest North American athlete of the 20th century by ESPN. Do you think that would have been the case if he had been on the basketball court by himself? Probably not. Although he was the leader on that team, he heavily depended on his team to lift him up.

Richard Branson runs multiple companies with great success. He depends on and recognizes the importance of people and puts them first. He knows that he is only one person and that ignoring the contributions of those around him would limit his success. He's a perfect example of somebody that would lose much of what he has if he forgot the importance of those around him, so instead he always puts them first.

Branson recognizes the value of building relationships with people and I can promise you he is a master at it. In order to run all of Virgin's subsidiaries with the success they have, he couldn't possibly focus on the daily operations of each individual company. Instead, he focuses on each of the individuals running those companies. He ultimately creates trusting relationships with them through great leadership, and in turn, they lead their individual companies with great leadership.

What all of these great leaders would agree on is that other people will play the most important role in any leader's success and the true secret to getting anywhere in life is your ability to connect with the people around you.

We are not in this world alone. We depend on others in every aspect of our being. And although dealing with people can be one of the most challenging problems you face, it can also be the most rewarding.

Understand that as a leader, your level of success will be determined by how well you communicate, react, and respond to everyone around you. In order to communicate, react, and respond effectively, you need to understand yourself and take the time to understand others. Once you figure out what drives other people, you can motivate them to succeed. If you learn to match other people's strengths with areas that you find challenging, you can accomplish great things.

Learning to work with and motivate others means understanding that you cannot change people. You are in control of one person and that person is *you*. No matter what you do, you can't force anyone to think a certain way, or act a certain way. Only they can decide to do that for themselves. What you can do, however, is connect with them so that they want to help you and they want you to be successful. Then you can motivate them into action using their strengths.

As business owners, managers and even as parents, you may often feel that you have earned the right to tell others what to do. And while that may be true in some respects, it is still up to that person to respond in a manner that supports your goals. So although it is not up to you how other people act and how they respond to you, you can still change how they are likely to be and how engaged they are.

The key is to get people to want to make decisions that will support you and your success. It is your responsibility as a leader to build strong relationships, to inspire others, and to get them to buy in to you and your vision. To do this, you must understand where the true power lies: in the hands of those around you.

So now that you know what you need to do to be successful, how will you know if you're ready to make these changes? Are you ready to start putting others above yourself and connecting with those around you?

In *Winning with People,* John Maxwell gives us 5 questions[4] to ask to help us understand if we are prepared for relationship building:

1. Are you prepared for relationships?

2. Are you willing to focus on others?

3. Can you build a mutual respect?

4. Are you willing to invest in others?

5. Can you create a win-win relationship?

Once you've established that you are ready and able to start building strong and meaningful relationships with others, you are ready to start connecting with people on another level. The next step will be to learn about those around you, recognize what drives them, and begin to adapt your behavior to allow for deeper connections. If you are ready to do that then I would say Onward to being purposeful in building these relationships in all areas of your life.

"Few are those who see with their own eyes and feel with their own hearts."

–Albert Einstein

Chapter 2

Don't Compare Yourself to Others

Let's get real with the fact that we all tend to compare ourselves in some way or another with other people. You see somebody doing well in their career and think you're not doing well enough. You see somebody in much better shape and feel bad about your fitness routine. You watch somebody create an awesome business and you feel stuck in an office. You watch people travel the world, learn languages, go to exotic places, and stay at amazing resorts and think your life is not near as glamorous, or you're not as successful.

It's human nature to compare yourself to others. It's natural, but it can be harmful to your self-esteem and hinder your motivation. Comparing yourself with those around you can be an unhealthy habit. We are all very different in the way we think, the way we process information, and the way we interpret things. Everyone has different experiences and feels different emotions. While some people work toward nice vacations or physical fitness, you may have different goals, and a different focus in your life.

Once you realize every person has a different personality style, you can see the value that everyone brings to the table individually. A variety of strengths, goals, and ideas can be beneficial to any individual or team. Each person will have a different set of skills and strengths and by recognizing these strengths and learning from them, everyone can grow together.

The moment you revert back to comparing yourself, you can start to self-destruct as there will always be people who you see as smarter, more successful, or generally better than you. Comparing yourself to others rather than valuing your unique qualities can lead to thoughts of worthlessness, animosity, and jealousy, none of which will help you achieve your goals.

Social norms dictate that we look a certain way, and act a certain way. However, each of us brings a unique personality and set of skills to the relationships we have. As such, we should embrace the ways in which we are different. Understanding yourself and the aspects of your personality that make you different, will help you in appreciating the diversity of others, and taking a step toward building more effective relationships.

Getting to know *you* and your strengths, and recognizing areas for improvement is not about comparing yourself to someone else. We all have room for improvement; nobody is completely flawless, whether it is on the outside or on the inside. While some people may have strengths you value, the opposite is true as well, you have strengths where others may fall short.

The goal of this book is for you to recognize the importance of understanding who you are and that you have a lot to offer. Rather than comparing yourself to others, recognize your own strengths and opportunities to grow. At the same time, though, you have to make a clear distinction that learning from other people is an important part of critical decision-making and personal development. In doing this you are not comparing, but rather evaluating where others succeed in order to establish opportunities to build your skills and abilities through them.

The idea is to appreciate your own strengths and improve yourself, not to impress other people, but because it will make you a much happier and successful person.

You have to recognize that we are all very different people, with different traits, in different circumstances, within different groups, and in different lives. Everyone has a different idea of success, and a different view of how to get there. When you think of it this way, there are very few things that you can actually compare. You wouldn't compare the taste of a pizza to a big juicy steak; you couldn't because they are not similar.

So your opportunity here is to enjoy your life, learn about who *you* are, accept the people around you, learn from them, and enjoy the journey.

Who Do I Want to Be?

There comes a time in everyone's life when you start looking towards a bigger picture. You begin to see things from a different perspective and start a process of self-discovery. This happens to some of us earlier in life than others, but most of us experience it at some point or another.

You begin to realize that hoping and waiting for someone or something to miraculously change is probably not going to happen. You stop believing that happiness, security and complete satisfaction in life will just magically happen to you. There comes a time that you come to realize that *you* need to stop waiting for things to happen for you, and start taking control of the direction and purpose of your life.

If you accept that everybody is entitled to their opinion, it is easier to understand that not everyone will always love, appreciate, or approve of who you are in every situation. There is no one universal embodiment of perfection. You may never be who everyone thinks you should be. Who you are and the way you behave in life is a result of conditioning you have received since birth. A lifetime of conditioning will not be changed quickly or easily, but you do have the power to choose who you want to be.

Recognize the good in yourself and be ready to shed the bad. Changing your behavior or conditioning can be much like the turning of a cruise ship, slow and steady until you are heading the direction you want to be going, then full throttle.

It begins with appreciating and loving who you are, developing confidence in yourself, and recognizing that you have tremendous value to others. This is not about being egotistical, but rather, it's about being assured that who you are matters. Developing an ego will only cause anger, jealously and resentment which can suffocate you and become a poison to those around you. Be sure to always keep it in check, and remember that there should be a balance between appreciating what you bring to the table, and the humility that allows you to recognize what others bring as well.

Once you realize it will not make anything better to complain or blame other people for what they've done or not done, you become accountable for finding solutions. Life isn't always fair, so there will be many times when you need to find a solution for a problem you haven't created. However, understand that it's not always somebody else's fault either, and that blaming and complaining will not make you well loved, and will not help you achieve your goals.

When you stop judging and pointing fingers, you begin to accept people as they are. You can overlook others' shortcomings and start recognizing your own. You will stop trying to control people and start to appreciate things as they are. If somebody blames you or takes their dissatisfaction out on you, don't take it personally; in most situations it tends to be more their issue than yours.

However, when you can admit when you are wrong, and take responsibility of the things that happen around you, you begin to build bridges rather than walls. It's much easier to cross bridges than to be constantly climbing walls. If you take responsibility for yourself and your actions, and understand that you get in life what you believe you deserve, you can start to see better outcomes.

Where you are in life is due to the choices you have made or the choices someone else has made for you. Most people refuse to take responsibility for their outcomes, but this does not have to be the way you are. Instead, you can decide to make a change in your life. You can choose to take responsibility for your life and your success, and you can *choose* your lot in life.

If you are open to change and willing to accept different points of view, you can reassess and redefine who you are and what you believe in. By redefining who you are to others, you may find a whole new level of how to connect with people and solidify relationships.

"Whatever you hold in your mind will tend to occur in your life. If you continue to believe as you have always believed, you will continue to act as you have always acted. If you continue to act as you have always acted, you will continue to get what you have always gotten. If you want different results in your life or your work, all you have to do is change your mind."

–Unknown

Chapter 3

What's This All About?

When you're ready to understand and accept that your success depends on the choices and decisions you make and the relationships you build, and take responsibility for the success or failure of these relationships, you will be ready for the changes that are about to happen. In order to do this, you will need to understand the impact of your thoughts and your ability to control your outcomes, and how two sides of your brain function and impact your behavior.

On one side, our subconscious represents approximately 95-99% of our cognitive activity. As individuals, we are not aware of this activity, but it greatly influences our personalities and habits. I like to refer to this as our natural behavior. We are born with many of our subconscious behaviors, passed on from generation to generation. Others have developed from the environment we grew up in, and from a regular pattern of conscious decision.

On the other side, our conscious mind represents the remainder of our cognitive activity (1-5%). This is where we reason and draw conclusions. Our conscious mind activates our imagination and controls our choices and willpower. I like to think of this as our chosen behavior. This side of our mind can be very powerful as our conscious decisions can create new programming for the subconscious mind and natural behavior over time. This is key when trying to change internal personality conflicts.

Our subconscious mind activates our immediate reactions and reflexes. We usually think of this as happening *without thinking*. It can be what saves us from dangerous situations, but it can also cause us to be self-sabotaging and self-limiting. This natural reflex can be very dangerous when developing relationships until we become aware of it and are willing to make necessary changes.

Our conscious mind, on the other hand, allows us to recognize and control our responses. Conscious thought can counteract unconscious activity and help us to recognize when we are self-sabotaging or self-limiting. By conditioning our conscious thought, we can work toward living a purposeful life with focused choices and decisions; ultimately reprogramming our subconscious mind.

There is always a place for both subconscious and conscious thought, though. I like to think of them as the difference between reacting, where you take quick, uncontrolled action, and responding, where you take the time to process information and make controlled decisions.

Here's an example. Sit back and relax. I want you to slowly read the next few paragraphs while picturing it in your head.

Put your hand out and imagine that you are holding a lemon. The lemon is bright yellow and you can smell the zest of the lemon just by holding it. You take out a knife and cut the lemon in half. You feel the lemon juice running between your fingers.

Imagine tipping your head back with your mouth wide open, now begin to squeeze the lemon, you can feel the juice running down your hand and into your mouth. You feel the juice pour into your mouth and you can taste the sourness of the juice on your tongue. It tastes so sour that your eyes crinkle.

Is your mouth watering yet? Is the lemon real? No, but your conscious mind told your unconscious mind a story that ultimately caused your body to react as if it was really happening. Your mouth watering is out of your control.

Can you imagine if you could learn to control how your unconscious mind causes your body to react in every situation? Once you can learn to manage your decisions through your conscious mind and then begin to program your brain with the right stuff, you can master your every behavior.

In your daily life, you rely on both your conscious and subconscious mind. Your personality is created over years within your subconscious mind but it can be controlled and curbed by your conscious mind. Most of us do not understand how to take control, so we often revert to subconscious reactions to negative situations, rather than conscious responses.

Problems arise when your subconscious mind takes the driver's seat. Immediate reactions can often be taken as short-sighted and rude. If you allow your subconscious to dictate your actions without filtering through your conscious mind, others may find you difficult to deal with. Your conscious mind allows you to strategize and plan for outcomes. When you ensure this side is activated, you have more control over how you respond to situations and how you talk to people, usually making you easier to deal with.

There is an old saying, "It's just how I'm wired." Many people use this idea to justify their behavior. But while the way you're wired does have something to do with your behavior, it does not have to be the determining factor. Ultimately, you can purposefully choose how you respond to any situation based on an understanding of your natural behavior and other people's natural behavior. It is up to you to decide how the two will interact.

When you live a purpose-driven life, you understand how you are wired. You can influence outcomes by maintaining control of aspects of your personality that inhibit your ability to deal with others. By employing your conscious mind, you can build relationships effectively and get your natural behavior in check.

Many of us look at the behaviors of others and judge them. Are they good or bad? Are they strengths or weaknesses? And we often do this with ourselves as well. Each of us has great strengths and areas that may challenge us. In order to avoid roadblocks to building relationships, we need to recognize the areas that may be holding us back.

Once you understand your natural tendencies and focus your effort through your conscious mind, you begin living your life on purpose. You will ultimately hold the power to create strong meaningful relationships.

Although your conscious mind only controls a small portion of your cognitive activity, it can be powerful enough to program your subconscious mind and change your natural behaviors and thoughts. Which will then change your outlook, curb your behavior, and help you make better decisions.

They say what you put into your brain is what you will get out. In other words, what you consciously put into your brain will eventually become your unconscious reality. This is important as your unconscious mind often controls how you feel and how you react to situations.

Once you are able to put this into practice, you will begin to truly master *you*.

Paradigm Shift

In *The 7 Habits of Highly Effective People*,[5] Stephen Covey explains that in order to make significant change, people must go through a *paradigm shift*; a change in their outlook on the world. You may have already experienced a paradigm shift in your life or you still may, as you change your way of seeing the world. Your paradigm shift might very well be your realization that you can make changes in the way you act and interact with people to change the results you've been getting. No matter when your moment is, your paradigm shift will change the way you see the world and your role within it.

Let me illustrate Dr. Covey's experience.

On a Sunday morning, Dr. Covey got on a subway in New York. It was a very quiet morning with only a few other passengers in the car. Most were reading the newspaper and keeping to themselves.

At one stop, the door opened and a man with several children boarded the subway. The children were so loud and causing a ruckus that the climate within the car instantly changed.

The man sat right next to Dr. Covey and did absolutely nothing about the behavior of his children. They became increasingly disruptive, throwing things and grabbing at people's paper. It was at this point that Dr. Covey decided to speak up. He turned to the man and asked him to do something about his children's behavior.

When he spoke, the other man raised his head and looked around at what his kids were doing. He said, "I'm sorry, I guess I should. We are just on our way back from the hospital and their mother just died about an hour ago. I guess I just don't know what I am going to do and they probably don't know how to handle it either."

Take a second to reflect on that situation. Can you see how suddenly the situation changed? A quick shift from being frustrated and angry to sympathetic and understanding in a matter of seconds.

This is just an example of how your attitude and your behavior can change in any given situation just by better understanding the whole story, or by looking at it from a different perspective. In order to change habits and behaviors created over your lifetime, you will have to extrapolate from this story, and start training your conscious mind. It will take time and purposeful effort to establish a life-long shift in your perspective.

Remember that it isn't what *actually* happens to us that necessarily will affect our behavior, but our *interpretation* of what happens to us. If you can change the way you react or view any given situation, you are on a path to significant change and new habits for adapting and dealing with people.

Now, you can combine your openness to see things differently with your understanding of how your subconscious mind can impact your behaviors and actions. The idea is that you can use your conscious mind to help program new behaviors. By putting this all together, you will start to live purposefully, adapt to those around you, and begin the journey to developing strong meaningful relationships that will help you succeed.

Where are You?

As you continue to grow and mature, there are a few phases you'll go through. One of these phases is realizing the important role others play in your level of success. Unfortunately, there are some people that never recognize it.

***

I was sitting in my office when one of the administrative assistants in my workplace knocked on the door and asked to speak with me. She works for a woman who is known to be cold and demanding.

She began her conversation with me by saying, "I don't know what I am supposed to do. I want to keep this job but she can't keep treating me this way. I don't deserve to be spoken to like that." The truth is that nobody does.

She continued by reading an email she was sent in which her boss degraded and insulted her. She finished the email by asking her to be more on the ball and threatening to fire her. Instead of making her want to step up, she actually just wanted to step out.

This woman had gone through three administrative assistants in the past year and was in a constant mode of frustration and turmoil. She didn't understand the value of people and she definitely did not take responsibility for her role in her relationship with her assistant.

***

If this is you or somebody you know, you are probably reading the right book. If you are constantly starting over with new relationships, there is a good chance you need to look in the mirror and take responsibility for your behavior.

Throughout life, you are dependent on other people. When you were a child, you were fully dependent on your parents for food, shelter, and protection. As you age, you find that you depend on people in different ways. When you mature into adulthood, there comes a point when you realize you can now do most things for yourself.

Eventually, as you become more independent and able to take care of yourself, you forget your need for others. At some point, you probably had the attitude of "I can take care of myself" and "I do not need anybody else." While it is important to build self-reliance and self-confidence, the ultimate key to success and living a purpose-driven life is learning that you can only do so much on your own. You need to recognize the value in having others help you reach your full potential.

Dependent people fully rely on others to get what they want. Independent people get what they want through their own effort. The greatest level of success is reached when independent people take it to the next level by seeing the value of working with other people and trusting them to help you. In doing this, you can begin to shift toward valuing people and inspiring them to value you as well. With help from others, you will get further in life with less stress and more satisfaction.

Take Control

At this point you probably get it. Ultimately it's your responsibility to take control of your behavior and what happens to you. But it is your relationships with others that can create or limit the success you have in life. As humans it's our natural behavior to automatically blame others when something goes wrong. To be successful, you will need to start taking the blame, rather than dishing it out.

It doesn't have to always be *their* fault, or *they* did this. Very rarely do people react with "it's me," or "if I only did that." And although it may be true that someone or something else played a role in the issue, most of the time the real problem is how you react. It's up to you to take responsibility of what has happened and resolve it.

We often think that blaming others or expecting others to change will resolve all of our challenges. So although it seems easier to blame others or try to get them to act differently and make better decisions, the truth is that we need to take control of the only person we can: ourselves. You can only make choices for yourself; you will never be able to control the choices of others, no matter your position in life.

C. Edwards

When you stop trying to control other people and get in control of yourself, you will see a huge improvement in your relationships with your co-workers, your kids, your friends, your spouse, and even the guy at the fast food restaurant that keeps messing up your order.

It's amazing how mastering just this one area of your life can create better opportunities, a greater level of happiness, more satisfaction with yourself, and stronger relationships.

As a society, we are very quick to judge other people and become self-proclaimed experts on other people's behavior. But when we are told to look in the mirror we have an uncanny ability to only see what we do right. We don't often consider that the outcome of any event in life can be managed by our own reactions so we automatically look to other people or outside influences for solutions.

Once you become aware of *who* you are and *how* you behave, you can begin to control your emotional reactions. Then you begin to purposefully respond in a way that allows other people to understand where you are going and what you are doing.

If done correctly, you quickly learn how your behavior and responses shape how others respond to you, and the decisions they make. What's important to remember is that you should not respond in a way that matters to you but rather in a way that matters to the other person. You then begin to speak their language, not your own. In doing this, you can communicate with people so they understand you on a level they can relate to. Then you start to build stronger, more meaningful relationships with people in your life.

Not only will you develop stronger relationship with people, but you will be able to reach your goals through them.

***

One day, I came into the office very focused on a project. I walked in the door and straight to my office to get the day rolling.

At the end of the day, I heard a knock and a quiet voice asking for a minute of my time. I said, "Sure come on in." It was my assistant, and I could tell she was upset. I asked what was wrong and she said to me, "I just wanted to come in and apologize if I did something wrong. Although, I don't know what I did to upset you."

My surprised response was, "Nothing at all, you are always amazing!"

"Well, this morning when you came in you looked angry, you didn't stop to even say good morning, and you've gone all day without saying a word to me. I feel like I did something wrong and I'm sorry!"

I was taken aback as she was the best assistant I'd ever had. She always did an amazing job, and I was definitely not upset with her at all. As the conversation continued, I found out she was worried all day because she thought she was going to lose her job. I respected her and what she did for me and I completely trusted her to make all the decisions that day, which is why I hadn't felt the need to say anything to her. We saw the day completely differently.

To me, I was focused on a big project and never thought that I may have been treating her in a way that made her feel insecure. To her, the way I treated her caused her to go through the entire day worrying about what she did wrong and if she was going to lose her job. While I remained focused and accomplished my goal, she couldn't because she was worried and distracted.

The lesson in that for me was that no matter how focused I am every day, I still need to take the time to recognize people and communicate with them in a way that works for them and that they understand. If I want to be effective in any relationship, it is my job to be aware of what I need to do to create a positive environment. After that day I never missed stopping to say good morning!

***

In order to move forward with mastering relationships, you have to understand your strengths as well as the challenges you face that may hold you back.

First, you need to understand that neither your strengths nor your weaknesses are good or bad. Having a strength in one area does not make you superior nor does a weakness make you inferior. Assessing these areas simply allows you to understand where you naturally focus when pursuing goals and success, and allows you to recognize the aspects of yourself that may be more difficult to overcome and things you may need to avoid.

We all have areas of weakness that challenge us, however these areas do not have to hold us back. In order to succeed, what you need to focus on is being purposeful in managing those areas so they do not cause roadblocks in your success.

There will be many people you cross paths with that you can relate to based on your strengths as well as your weaknesses. You cannot avoid people that you don't relate well with and you cannot expect people to bend to relate to you. So you need to make an effort to find ways to relate to others – drawing on both your strengths and your weaknesses will help you adapt.

To understand others, you first need to understand yourself. It takes at least two people to have a conversation and you'll face challenges until you learn to manage yourself first. So, the next step in successfully mastering relationship building is to get to know who you are and be open to learning about yourself. Acknowledge the good and accept your imperfections. Remember, how people see you will always remain more important than how you see yourself, and what they see is the way you behave.

Perception vs. Reality

Several years ago, I took part in my first personality profile. It was part of the hiring process for a new job. The profile report had a section called Perceptions. It assessed both self-perception, and others' perceptions of you. The report indicated that I saw myself as pioneering, competitive, positive, assertive, confident and a winner, all of which made sense to me. I assumed it was also how everyone else saw me.

It was the next part that gave me a huge slap to the ego and made me re-evaluate who I am. Right below the self-perception was a list of words of how *other* people perceived me: demanding, egotistical, nervy, aggressive, abrasive, controlling, and opinionated.

My first thought was, "How dumb is this profile!" However, the longer I thought about it and the more I reflected on my life's experiences, things started to come together. It was then that I had to decide whether or not I would admit the report could be right and make a decision to hear what it was telling me. I decided that this was NOT how I wanted people to see me, and that I would need to make some adjustments.

It took some time, but eventually I realized I needed to understand *why* people perceived me this way. I would need to make changes in how I communicate and treat people, in order to change their perceptions.

Since then I have made a huge change for the better and my life has taken a turn. I've realized life becomes much easier and much more rewarding when people respect and like you, and when people want to be around you.

***

So what is reality? And what is perception? When our perception differs so much from person to person, can anything be considered universally true? Although this philosophical question is beyond the scope of this book, the difference between reality and perception matters greatly in building relationships with people. There are so many variables that determine why someone connects with someone else.

Your version of what is real is only your *perception* of reality, not what is universally true. This was a huge eye opener for me. What I quickly learned was just because you see something a particular way does not make it the absolute truth. While it may be true to you, others' perceptions are much more important to building relationships. How you think others look at you is just your version of reality, or your *perception*. How you see others is often a reflection of who you are as a person and how you see yourself.

Often, people can be so insistent that their way of thinking about and understanding people and problems is more accurate or true than someone else's. This is how I was before the profile report. For me, it often caused problems because the people around me perceived me as difficult to work with and not willing to be a team player.

When evaluating yourself and considering others' perceptions, you'll have to keep an open mind and remember that a person's point of view is *always* valuable, whether it is about an issue on the table or about an individual on the team. Remember you and your views are also being scrutinized by the people you surround yourself with.

How you view things or what you determine as real is defined by your belief structure. Your belief structure determines your perception, which ultimately determines how you respond to events and people. The great part about your beliefs is that you can choose to examine them and make changes accordingly.

You may not be in control of what happens to you in your life and who you meet along the way, but you can certainly take control of how you respond. That part is in your control and ultimately allows you to shape your reality and others' perceptions of you as well.

There is a lot involved in how people perceive you. Your body language, actions, verbal communication, and even your appearance. Slouching during meetings or crossing your arms may show you're not interested and that you're not open to what's going on. People may think you're obnoxious if you speak in a loud, strong voice or are always in control of a conversation. Even the way you dress and how you carry yourself creates a perception that often causes people to treat you differently.

It doesn't matter if you think their perceptions are right or wrong. You can only control how you choose to see things, and influence how others might perceive you. So what they perceive to be true can become their reality, despite how much you may disagree. When trying to build relationships and communicate with other people, it is their perception of you and the situation they are in that needs to matter most to you, even if you think it may be distorted.

You may believe that people see you as you see yourself, but I had to learn the hard way that this is simply not true.

To change how others perceive you, you will have to learn how your actions, body language, and verbal communication influence perceptions. First, you have to examine yourself and be open to make necessary change. Then, you need to minimize the gap between how you see yourself and the perception others have of you.

Understand that you will never be able to change everyone's perception, and I would not suggest you to aim to please others at the expense of your dignity. There is a fine line between getting people to see the real you and conforming only to what you think people want and expect from you. However, you must always understand that how others see you directly affects how they feel about you and act toward you. If you want to change that, you'll need to change their perception.

Changing perceptions is not about changing your character or who you are, but rather understanding yourself and showing who you are to others in a way that *they* can see who you really are.

"Seeking out people with different views, different perspectives, different ideas is often challenging, because it requires us to set aside judgment and open our minds. But we have to remind ourselves that to get beyond where we are, where I believe most of us are, we would all be be well served to choose our music carefully, to stop talking and listen to one another."

–Susan Scott

Chapter 4

Understanding Each Other

Have you ever said something to a group of people and each individual took it completely differently? Have you ever been so misunderstood that it caused an argument? What you say and how other people understand it is based on who you are and who they are. As you know, every individual has their own unique personality. Not everyone thinks the same way, nor do they always act the way you want or expect.

In situations like these, we often find ourselves asking "Why did they say that?", "What were they thinking?", or "Why would they do that?" In order to understand others, and ensure others understand you, you'll have to embrace everyone's differences. You'll also need to figure out a way to better understand people who differ from you.

It takes all kinds of personalities to make the world go 'round. If we were all only good at the same few things, we would rarely accomplish anything. However, these differences and lack of understanding are also what can cause miscommunication, hurt feelings, and poor relationships.

Often, we find that these negative experiences cause a disconnect between coworkers, within families, and among friends. This can often lead to a breakdown in relationships and poor performance at work. Each employee might have the same skills and knowledge required for the position, but they may not be able to get along with each other. This in itself can cause big issues.

If you don't take time to understand how other people think and act, and why they behave a certain way, you may find yourself building walls with people. Not taking time to consider others could destroy your relationships.

We all process information and situations differently. The good news is that there is a way to help understand people and their behavior. In understanding personality profiles, we can start to understand what motivates others and the perspectives they bring to the table. In turn, this will allow you to reduce conflict, improve relationships, create positive environments, and relate to others in ways that will be more effective.

Personality Profiling

Although not a perfect science, personality profiling can help you quickly and easily categorize people into personality types. These personality types provide a way to generate a basic understanding of what drives each individual around us. Once you understand the types, you'll be able to better recognize and understand others. An added benefit is that you will also be able to classify yourself, and better understand what you prefer and why you act the way you do.

Using personality profiles, you will be able to recognize strengths and areas for improvement, and quickly recognize the behavior of others so you know how to best relate with them. These personality profiles are just the first step in building better relationships. Over time, you will need to engage with people and learn more about them as an individual, however understanding the differing personality profiles will help you get your foot in the door.

Imagine this:

You arrive at a meeting a few minutes late. As you walk into the room, you're greeted by a huge smile and a loud, friendly "Good morning! How are you doing?" That's Isobel, always positive and welcoming. At the other end of the table, you see David, another one of your colleagues. He is visibly upset that you've arrived late and starts rushing everyone to get started and get the meeting over with. About 10 minutes into the meeting, you notice Samantha hasn't said anything. She looks nervous about the discussion, so you ask what she thinks. "I don't think there's anything wrong with the way we've been doing it, why do we need a change?" David grumbles, and you remind everyone that these changes will boost productivity. She nods and says quietly, "Okay, as long as we all work on this together." Throughout the meeting, you've noticed Chris has been taking notes but not contributing much to the conversation. You ask for his input so he brings up his concerns about the viability of your plan and how you'll be able to implement it.

Each of these people responds differently to the given situation. A successful group or team will need all of these different perspectives and approaches. In dealing with people and building relationships, you'll need to know who on your team fits into which category to effectively work with each of them.

Personality profiling has been around for decades, but it is only in recent years that people have started to recognize it as an effective tool in helping understand and manage people.

There are numerous profiling methods. You've likely heard of the the Myers Briggs Type Indicator (MBTI), the Activity Vector Analysis (AVA) or DISC assessments. Each of these profiling types analyzes aspects of an individual's daily activity and thought process to categorize them into a group.

MBTI[6] uses a 16-type system to provide a very detailed description of each person's strengths, weaknesses, thought processes and interaction preferences. While it can be very helpful, especially when understanding yourself, it is not easy to recognize any one individual's personality type based on your interactions with them.

AVA[7] is a personality typing system that analyzes how people function in a work environment. It assesses behavioral tendencies and how an individual might fit into a specific job or function within your organization. It places people on 4 different spectra, including aggressiveness, sociability, emotional control, and social adaptability. The AVA can be an incredibly useful tool for job placement and coaching.

DISC, then, is a personality profiling system that allows you to place individuals on two intersecting spectra: how they deal with people, and how they manage tasks. It works for our purposes because it simplifies the process and allows us to recognize personality types quickly. It also indicates how we can work together and interact more effectively with each type.[8]

The DISC model of behavior was first proposed by William Mouton Marston in the 1920's. In his 1928 book, *Emotions of Normal People,* Marston explains the theory that normal human emotions lead to behavioral differences among groups of people. His work focused on directly observable and measurable psychological phenomena. Marston theorized that people are motivated by two intrinsic drives that impact behavioral patterns. Around 1948, Walter V. Clarke built an assessment instrument using Marston's theories.[9]

The personality profiling system outlined in this book is based on the DISC assessment as our focus is primarily the ways in which people interact and how we can assess personalities through observation in order to more effectively work with people and build relationships.

The simplicity of DISC's 4 categories enables you to broadly place people within these categories before getting to know them on a deeper level. You can easily and quickly make a broad assessment within minutes of meeting someone.

There are two primary behavioral factors to consider when profiling personalities using a DISC model: how they interact with others, and how they interact with tasks. How people interact with others can be classified along an Outgoing-Reserved spectrum. On the outgoing extreme, people tend to seem as though they are always 'switched on' or ready to 'dive in.' They can be interpreted as pushy or forceful in their communication as they are quick to engage with people and are often very chatty and interactive.

On the reserved extreme, people tend to be slow to act and extremely cautious in what they do. They don't often offer comments or initiate conversations, preferring to keep to themselves or be asked questions. This can often be interpreted as disinterest, but more often than not, they just prefer to observe. This spectrum is a sliding scale between the extremes. Everyone fits in somewhere.

How people interact with tasks can be considered along a Task-oriented-People-oriented spectrum. Extremely task-oriented people are often very focused on the task at hand. They have little time for interacting or working with others, as they prefer to just get the job done and move on to the next one. Socializing can be challenging for these people, and is typically not a priority for them.

On the other extreme, those who are people-oriented tend to focus on other people rather than the task at hand. Often, these individuals are well known in a social group, and people know when they walk into a room. They thrive on being in groups, but often have difficultly focusing on tasks and projects. Again, this is a sliding scale where everyone falls somewhere between these extremes.

Both behavioral factors are external qualities, so they are often very easy to assess or notice in others without spend-

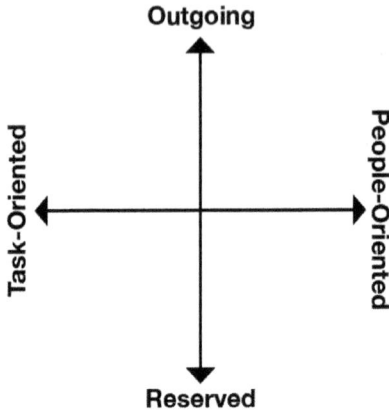

Outgoing

```
                    Outgoing
                        ▲
                        │
   Task-Oriented  ◄──────┼──────►  People-Oriented
                        │
                        ▼
                    Reserved
```

ing too much time analyzing people or administering tests. This makes it easy to better understand the people around you and begin to determine how they might prefer to be communicated with.

Of course, as these are both sliding scales, where we place on these spectra depends on many factors including our genes, the environment we are in, and our behavioral tendencies. Most people lean to one end of each spectrum, and very rarely does anyone find that they fit directly in the center. Your balance between these tendencies shapes the way you approach your daily life and those around you.

None of these preferences can or should be considered good or bad. They just are. So try to avoid passing judgment. Just because someone might be different than you, or differ greatly among your group of colleagues, does not mean they are any less capable or less integral to your team.

Personality Types

Using DISC, we classify people based on both spectra together, leaving us with four personality types:

- Decisive (upper left): outgoing and task-oriented
- Interactive (upper right): outgoing and people-oriented
- Supportive (lower right): reserved and people-oriented
- Cautious (lower left): reserved and task-oriented

In the situation described above, David is outgoing and task-oriented (Decisive). He is focused on getting through the meeting and moving on to the next task. Isobel is outgoing and people-oriented (Interactive). She made sure to welcome you and generally displays a positive attitude. Samantha is reserved and people-oriented (Supportive). She dislikes change, but will do what's best for the group. She likes working together to solve problems. Finally, there's Chris. He is reserved and task-oriented (Cautious). He doesn't like to speak up, but he is always concerned about getting the job done correctly.

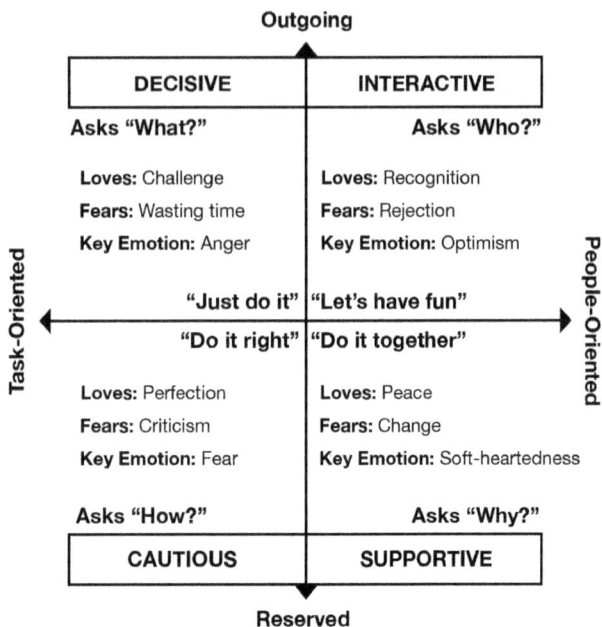

```
                        Outgoing
                           ▲
        ┌──────────────────┼──────────────────┐
        │    DECISIVE      │   INTERACTIVE    │
        └──────────────────┼──────────────────┘
        Asks "What?"              Asks "Who?"

        Loves: Challenge          Loves: Recognition
        Fears: Wasting time       Fears: Rejection
        Key Emotion: Anger        Key Emotion: Optimism

                  "Just do it" │"Let's have fun"
    ◄─────────────────────────┼─────────────────────────►
                  "Do it right"│"Do it together"

        Loves: Perfection         Loves: Peace
        Fears: Criticism          Fears: Change
        Key Emotion: Fear         Key Emotion: Soft-heartedness

        Asks "How?"              Asks "Why?"
        ┌──────────────────┼──────────────────┐
        │    CAUTIOUS      │   SUPPORTIVE     │
        └──────────────────┼──────────────────┘
                           ▼
                        Reserved
```

Task-Oriented (left axis) — People-Oriented (right axis)

Decisive

Decisive personalities fall on the outgoing and task-oriented ends of the spectra. They are often dominant doers. These individuals like a challenge and are focused on making things happen, accomplishing tasks, and getting results. Respect and results help in developing a strong relationship with people of this type.

Interactive

Interactive personalities fall on the outgoing and people-oriented ends of the spectra. They are often people who are expressive, inspiring, and influential. These individuals tend to be social, enjoy being in crowds, and want everything to be fun. They are concerned with how others see them, and this tends to drive them to be better. Recognizing and admiring them helps in developing a strong relationship with people of this type.

Supportive

Supportive personalities fall on the reserved and people-oriented ends of the spectra. They are primarily amiable, steady, and stable. These individuals enjoy building relationships, helping and supporting others, and working together on a team. They are very friendly people and expect the same of others. If you show sincere appreciation for what they do it will go far in building a strong relationship with people of this type.

Cautious

Cautious personalities fall on the reserved and task-oriented ends of the spectra. They are analytical, competent, and compliant. These individuals seek out value, consistency, and quality information. Being correct and accurate is a driving force for them. If you trust them and recognize their integrity, you can more easily build strong relationships with people of this type.

To access a **free** DISC personality assessment for yourself, visit **adaptthebook.com**

"To effectively communicate, we must realize that we are all different in the way we perceive the world and use this understanding as a guide to our communication with others."

–Tony Robbins

Chapter 5

Making it Work

Imagine how peaceful life would be if you only ever had to interact with people who see things the exact same way you do. Unfortunately, that would be incredibly boring and unproductive. Working and experiencing life with people who are completely different helps keep our own biases and preferences in check, and provides an ideal balance of extremes. So instead, we have to learn how to deal with a variety of personalities.

When working with others and building relationships, you need to ensure that you respect views from all types of people, and you work *with* them according to their strengths and preferences. Being a good leader and a good teammate means putting other people's preferences and biases ahead of yours to make those around you more comfortable and support others in their growth. Of course, you won't be giving up who you are, but rather adapting your behavior to the situations you find yourself in.

Many of us go through life playing the blame game when things don't go as planned. It is often difficult to look at negative situations and understand the role you've played in the outcome. When you can start to appreciate everyone's role, including your own, you can begin to take responsibility for the things that happen, and appreciate the need for people of differing personality strengths.

You should be looking critically at your role on the team. Understand that there are areas in which you could improve and develop. So rather than working against who you are, you can work with it. What you do with what you were given is what really matters.

In order to succeed and achieve your ultimate goals, you'll need to begin by learning who you are, understanding others, and then recognizing how you can best connect with people. Doing this will help you gauge how you should be working with others and responding to the people around you. It will also help you communicate to others how and why you prefer to be treated a certain way.

We often feel that we are who we are, and people should like us for that. I am not saying you should become someone else, but rather that you need to take responsibility for who you are and how that impacts and affects others. Be proactive in dealing with people as you only have one opportunity to make a good impression. This first impression will be what determines whether or not someone wants to take your relationship to the next level.

Understand that the problems you have with other people can directly stem from how you treat them and behave towards them. The problem, then, is actually yours not theirs. So, once you understand others, you'll need to understand how they perceive you. By being intentional in how you interact with them, you can often create a bond that may have not existed before. You'll need to learn to look at others and assess their key motivating factors, and in doing this, you will be able to connect with others more easily.

Managing Yourself

Now that you understand the basics of the DISC personality types, you can and must learn how to manage yourself in order to better relate to them. First, determine your own personality type, then recognize your personal strengths and challenges. Finally, understand how you must adapt to each personality to best relate to them.

Being aware of your personality type allows you to remain in control of your own behavior and your interactions with others. Base your decisions on how other people will respond, rather than how you want to communicate. This way, you will be able to build meaningful relationships faster and get further in life.

Decisive

As a Decisive personality, you are often direct, self-reliant, and competitive. You take risks and are focused on getting things done. You are quick-moving and always ready for a challenge.

Some areas of concern are your tendency to always be in a rush and forget to listen to what others say to you. Rather than just hearing what someone says, practice conceptualizing and responding to others' ideas and thoughts. Be careful that your body language is not too overpowering or aggressive. Rather than telling people what to do, try instead to suggest, recommend, or ask, and realize that most people will have their own way of completing tasks.

When others bring up their own ideas or solutions to you, be careful not to criticize. You may be sincere, joking, or just interested in the best for the team, but you can often come across as critical or negative. Although your confidence and self-assurance is a big part of who you are, it can often be perceived as arrogant and egotistical. It is not necessary to tell people how great you are; your light will shine through your actions and results.

Remember to listen and let others present their opinions and ideas before you offer yours, and respect their views. Be ready to offer suggestions and opinions, but be very careful in how you respond. Often, approaching a difficult topic may be easier if you ask questions rather than simply stating your opinion.

Interactive

As an Interactive personality, you know you are great at dealing with people, especially when it comes to influencing or persuading them. You prefer to express yourself verbally and may have high-risk ideas for projects that you're not willing to implement yourself.

In order to improve your communication with others, try to focus on listening and encouraging. Be careful not to talk too much, as you may be perceived as not caring. You are great at asking questions, so do more of that to help people perceive you as serious.

People enjoy the fact that you get excited and enthusiastic about things. Be sure that you do your research and investigate situations, ideas, and projects in advance. Find out all the information you'll need so as not to start a project that you won't be able to finish.

People who know you see you as an overly friendly person, which can often make those who don't know you uncomfortable or nervous. You thrive in situations with a lot of people and activity. Just remember that not everyone appreciates the same level of noise and excitement.

Supportive

As a Supportive personality, you are people-oriented, warm, and steady. This can be a great benefit when building relationships with others. Your strengths include cooperating with others and keeping the peace. You like to collaborate and achieve results together with your teammates. Your pace is systematic and methodical. Some may see it as too slow, but you complete high-quality work, so it is often worthwhile to take the time.

However, you need to be aware that there may be situations in which you'll need to speed things up, especially with your speech, gestures, and decision-making. Learn to present your ideas briefly and be ready to take action without as much warning as you may be comfortable with. Although you might be unsure in making decisions, be careful to stick to whatever you choose and not waiver.

For projects and tasks that require concentration and time, you will greatly exceed expectations so be sure to step up to the plate. This will help in pairing your natural strengths with your role on a team, making you an invaluable member.

Cautious

As a Cautious personality, you work to ensure quality and accuracy in all that you do and say. You are reserved and task-oriented, so you are very methodical and careful to avoid mistakes. You could describe yourself as detail-oriented. People often come to you for answers as they know you base decisions on facts and research. Your work is always meticulous and exceptional, although you often take extra time to complete tasks.

You take mistakes very seriously, so try to avoid being too critical when others make mistakes. When you provide feedback, be sure you are contributing to the bigger picture rather than getting lost in the details. Do your best to stay open to risky ideas and suggestions to ensure you are welcoming the ideas and suggestions of others.

Being too cautious can often cause you to blame or point the finger when things don't go the way you expect. Try to stay focused on reaching the main objective. Remember to ask yourself if you are helping the team in the long run. Being right is important to you, but sometimes you have to let go of that in order to move on to the next task and avoid arguments. There will be times when getting things done quickly will outweigh perfection, so be aware of time frames and deadlines.

Who's Who?

A relationship with any person is a dance. The only way to be sure to maintain a strong relationship is to be the one that takes full responsibility of the outcome. Just like in dancing, someone has to take the lead, otherwise you find yourself tripping over each other's feet.

In order to increase your effectiveness with people, it is important to understand how to manage your own behavior so it works with other personality types.

We have already learned that people can be characterized into these four basic personality styles:

- Decisive
- Interactive
- Supportive
- Cautious

Determining your own personality type is just the first step. You will now have to figure out who everyone else is and how they prefer to be interacted with, what they value in the personalities of others, and who they get along with best. Then, you can manage yourself to fit in with what works best in each situation.

Having a basic understanding of personality types, you can start to observe the people around you to figure out who they are. You might have already been doing this as you read through the descriptions. Here are some questions you might consider when observing others:

- Do they speak up often or do they seem to keep to themselves?
- Do they prefer to complete tasks quickly or take their time?
- Do you often know when they enter a room?
- Are they more often loud or do they tend to stay quiet?
- Do they get easily distracted or are they able to focus through commotion?
- Do they ever ask other colleagues to socialize after work?
- Are they friendly and kind to those around them or are they more critical?
- Do they always follow the rules and do what their superiors tell them?
- Do they vocalize their grievances or keep to themselves?
- Do they more often work in groups or alone?
- Are they detail-oriented?

You can also learn more about people by starting conversations with them. You don't have to ask them directly about their preferences, but you can, more often than not, figure out their preferences in general conversation. For example, when you talk to them, are they communicative or do they tend to keep to themselves?

When talking to people, try to pick up on some of these things:

- Do they complain or do they seem satisfied with everything around them?

- Do they speak quickly or do they think about what they are going to say?

- How do they respond when you provide feedback to them?

- How do they respond when you compliment them?

- Are they always trying to prove themselves right?

- Do they seem willing to talk with you during work hours, or do you sense they prefer when you leave them to their work?

- When you talk about yourself, do they listen or do they turn the conversation back to themselves?

- Are they supportive of your views or do they need to dominate conversation?

- Do they react better to you when you talk about doing projects quickly, or doing them correctly?

Working with Others

Each personality type has its own strengths and challenges. They vary greatly in what they consider to be high priority. Once you understand who you are, you can begin to figure out ways you can more easily and effectively work with other personalities. Understanding what people need and what they value can be crucial to communicating effectively and building better relationships.

The key is to first understand yourself and then recognize who others are so you can adapt your behavior around what they prefer and believe to be important. As you practice this more, you will become someone who values others and what they bring to the table. You will find that you can get much more accomplished with much less drama.

Here, we can examine how best to interact with each of these types:

Decisive

Decisive people like to take charge.

If you are also Decisive, understand that there cannot be two captains on the same ship. You will have to adjust your natural impulse to take charge, so as to allow others to feel comfortable taking or sharing that role. A key factor in this is to compromise. You may both want to take the lead, so perhaps you can share the responsibility or you can take a step back. As you, like other Decisive people, are competitive, make an effort to avoid talking down to others like you, and be conscious of treating them with a high degree of respect.

If you are not Decisive, be purposeful in your communication and understand that they prefer to work with people more like themselves. Make an effort to mirror some of their behaviors. While this may be uncomfortable, it can go a long way in connecting with someone of this type.

You will likely need to be more forward when presenting ideas to them, and you'll need to stand your ground when they challenge you. Do your best to avoid appearing unsure, hesitant, or tentative and demonstrate confidence through your body language and tone.

Decisive personalities prefer to have upfront and forward conversations. They prefer to communicate with people who are sure of themselves and who don't like to waste time. Because of this, make sure you are prepared for conversations with them. If it will help, try to write down some thoughts so you won't forget to discuss them.

Interactive

Interactive people like to be the center of attention.

If you are also Interactive, you may find yourself trying to control conversation and fighting for attention. This can cause communication issues and conflict. It will be very important to make sure you give each other time to speak, and to share the spotlight when necessary. Make an effort to sit back and listen rather than being the one controlling the conversation. Let somebody else take the lead.

You will find that you are both enthusiastic and fun people, and that you can get distracted easily when together. Be careful to stay on topic.

If you are not Interactive, you will need to remain conscious of their needs in order to build lasting and meaningful relationships.

Interactive personalities appreciate being appreciated, and enjoy when others are enthusiastic about their ideas. Make an effort to be optimistic when communicating with Interactive people. Your body language can say a lot to this person so make sure you are open and conscious of your facial expressions and vocal animations.

Interactive people prefer to be touchy-feely, to make eye contact, and to laugh or smile. If you tend to be quiet, this personality can often misinterpret you as disconnected or disinterested. Try to step outside your comfort zone and liven things up so they can more easily relate to you. Feel free to express your feelings to them as they will be there to support you. Doing this can help bring you closer together.

Although you may not relate to them, it's important that you appreciate them and treat them with respect, this alone will help you tremendously in building that tight bond.

Supportive

Supportive people prefer working together and helping others achieve their goals.

If you, too, are Supportive, you will likely feel more comfortable working with someone like you. However, this can often be counter-productive when you need to make decisions. Make an effort to be decisive when working with other Supportive people – not only will you be more productive, but they will appreciate not having to make the decisions. When working together to present ideas, try to set strict deadlines to ensure tasks are completed on time.

You are a natural peacekeeper, so when dealing with conflicts, don't sweep things under the rug; that is a sure way to cause more problems in the future. Eliminate problems by dealing with them now. Remember, another Supportive person may tend toward avoiding conflict as well. It is not, however, healthy for a long term relationship and may end in resentment.

If you are not predominantly Supportive, be careful when dealing with this personality type. Supportive people are often sensitive to being rushed and feeling like they are not appreciated. Be sure to exercise patience when working with them, as they are sure and steady in all that they do. If you rush them they may withdraw, so avoid being rash or irritable when things don't happen as quickly as you expected. Although making snap decisions may be the way to move forward, be careful not to seem impulsive or impatient.

When working with Supportive personalities, you will need to make an effort to acknowledge this person regularly. If you treat these people right, they can be your biggest allies, so it is worth the work to treat them the way they want to be treated.

Cautious

Cautious people like to get things done right the first time.

If you are also Cautious, working with someone like yourself can be easier, but it does come with its challenges. Often, when working with people like yourself, you can get caught up in the details and lose sight of the big picture. Make an effort to support each other to stay on track and focused in order to get things done.

Rules, systems, and policies are extremely important, but you can easily bury each other in procedure. As you are both perfectionists, you need to be careful not to be too critical or you risk negative backlash.

If you are not Cautious, you may feel that rules are just guidelines and systems are for the disorganized. You'll need to adjust your perspective and understand that rules and systems are quite important to a Cautious person. When dealing with people of this nature, make an effort to be on time and to appear to have everything in order. Otherwise, they may find you to be disrespectful.

When having discussions with Cautious people, research facts and get details together beforehand. Make an effort not to state facts unless you are sure they are accurate. Be prepared to be criticized and asked a lot of questions if they are not open to your ideas. Coming to them with facts and proven methods will always help in building a respect that will lead to stronger relationships.

What's Their Problem?

Now that you know who everyone is and how they prefer to be interacted with, you can start to understand where others are coming from and adapt yourself to be better

DECISIVE	INTERACTIVE
DO: Be clear, specific, brief Set goals for performance Be results-fucused **DON'T:** Be disorganized or lazy Talk too much Be indecisive	**DO:** Be warm and friendly Ask for opinions Give compliments **DON'T:** Be too detailed Criticize or ridicule Dominate conversation
CAUTIOUS	**SUPPORTIVE**
DO: Be prepared with facts Be accurate, precise Stick to the task **DON'T:** Appear disorganized Criticize Talk about irrelevant issues	**DO:** Be kind and understanding Ask about them Present problems softly **DON'T:** Rush them Be controlling, demanding Be insensitive, sarcastic

received by your colleagues, acquaintances, and friends. Unfortunately, not everyone will be easy to work with.

Regardless of personality type, there are many people who are generally very difficult to work with. You can, however, use the knowledge within these profiles to try to get on their good side and create a connection that will help you overcome their difficult behavior.

First, just like you have with other people around you, assess this person using the personality profiling information provided and by asking yourself questions about their behavior. Remember, you can do this through both observation and conversation. Once you understand their personality, you may be able to understand their behavior as well.

Use what you have learned about dealing with each personality type. Make your best effort to adapt and mirror their behavior to act in accordance with their preferences. Although you may not want to connect with this person, it is important to try to form a connection anyway.

Next, try to be proactive. If you notice someone's behavior has suddenly changed, or you have just met someone who is particularly difficult, try to start the process right away. Don't wait until you have already had several arguments or you already have hard feelings. Of course, this is not always possible, but when it is, it will be worthwhile to address the issue before the wall between you is too high to overcome.

Observe and converse as much as you can with anyone who is difficult, but recognize their boundaries and don't push it. Remember that some personalities like interacting with people, and others don't. Do your best to keep their preferences in mind while also trying to relate to them.

Throughout this process, remember what you have learned about each individual personality type. Everyone has preferences and ideas about how relationships should work

and how people should interact. They'll also have preferences in work styles and environments. Whenever possible, create an environment for that person in which they
will feel most comfortable.

When dealing with people who are particularly difficult,
remember that it is not likely you they have a problem
with. Although you might be their focus or the person
they blame, they are likely dealing with external factors
that affect their mood, their view of you, and your relationship. Be as understanding as possible, and try not to
take personal offense.

Finally, do what you can to communicate clearly. If the
situation or disagreement has become painful for you, or
if it makes your work life difficult, try to have a conversation with that person. It is possible they don't even realize
anything is wrong – maybe they don't understand how to
work with your personality type. Or perhaps they don't
understand how you feel or that you are willing to work
toward positive change. Communication is key to overcoming these obstacles.

Regardless of the situation, make an effort to communicate with the difficult person. Depending on your own
personality, this may be incredibly difficult. However, creating and building positive relationships with the people
around you can have a huge impact on your satisfaction at

work, and the success you achieve in your career and your life in general. Just try it, the outcome may surprise you.

"When you think everything is someone else's fault, you will suffer a lot. When you realize that everything springs only from yourself, you will learn both peace and joy."

–Dalai Lama

Chapter 6

The Power of Choice

Every day you will find yourself making choices that will affect every relationship you have. Every time you wake up next to your spouse in bed, pass a co-worker in the hall, or see a friend at the store, you face a decision that can carry real consequences. It is up to you to ensure your choices move these relationships in a positive direction.

The principles in this book are not about maintaining the status quo, they are in the interest of change for the better: to make different choices, powerful ones, that can drastically change your outcomes in life.

As the saying goes, "Insanity is doing the same thing over and over again and expecting different results." It applies to everything in life, including developing relationships with people. We all know somebody who has been in relationship after relationship, always blaming the other person for it ending, and rarely taking responsibility for the outcome. Frankly, they will continue that trend unless they are willing to do something different, to make a change in the way they treat others and relate to the people around them.

So it is in recognizing who you are and how you interact with people that you can see where changes need to be made. And it is these changes that define how your relationships develop and how successful you become.

It is easy to underestimate the power and influence you have in simple, causal encounters with people. Although they may seem mundane, these encounters can impact your relationships as much as any formal meeting or sit-down meal at home. While you may think you only influence relationships with major interactions, it is the the most trivial moments that can make all the difference. A simple 'hello' or smile when you see someone in the hallway has a huge impact on long-term relationship building. It is gestures like these that often become the foundational piece to establishing a relationship.

Your daily reactions and interactions can have the most immediate power to effect positive change. Recognizing your opportunities to make better choices starts with being aware of the opportunities around you and being willing to create change in your life and your relationships.

There will be times when it is tough for you to make the best choices, especially when viewpoints clash and tempers flare. Although most people tend to stop thinking and start reacting, your goal should be to remain calm in spite of your frustration, and to learn to respond thoughtfully rather than react rashly.

It's easy to get overwhelmed by the challenges you face in creating new habits and in overcoming obstacles. I can promise that you will see amazing results. When you can be purposeful enough to break the normal response habits that negatively affect your life, you will be surprised by the transformation you see in the relationships you have with others.

False Belief

As a Decisive person, admitting I need to make a change, and then actually making that change is something I really struggle with. My fascination with personalities began with the profile I brought up in Chapter 3. It was an eye-opening experience. I really liked myself but nobody else did!

There was a huge difference between how I perceived myself and how other people perceived me. I was devastated as I didn't want to be seen that way. I really thought I was amazing. Maybe not perfect, but at the very least not as bad as what the profile implied.

When I read the profile, the biggest struggle I had was that I didn't understand why there was such a wide gap between my self-perception and what others thought of me. My first thought was that there wasn't anything that I could do about it. It was who I was and changing that would be impossible.

I quickly came to recognize, however, that what I thought of myself didn't really matter to others, and that I would have to make some big changes to change their perception of me.

I began to look back on my life and see things differently. I examined my outcomes and how people treated me, and then I looked at how I treated others. Things started to add up and make more sense as I began to recognize how I could have done things differently. At that point, I decided I needed to figure out how to make a change.

Today, I still struggle with the same things I always have, but I am more aware of and purposeful in my actions, especially in the way I treat and deal with people. This has allowed me to create different, stronger, relationships with everyone in my life.

Many of us spend much of our time complaining about our problems and placing blame on others for the lot we've been given. We also tend to go through life expecting other people to treat us in a way that makes us happy. Many people don't understand when that doesn't work out. If in any relationship neither person takes responsibility for the outcome, it's easy and natural to place blame on others when things go bad.

When discussions get heated or turn negative, you can often see destructive behavior rise to the surface. You might use or hear language like, "Well, that's just the way I am!" which often leads down the path of "And I can't do anything about it," or "If it bothers you then that's too bad!" Once this starts it is clear that there has been a breakdown in communication.

The problem is, when you believe you can't change, you act according to your natural or subconscious behavior regardless of how it makes others feel. Such an attitude is absolutely limiting and destructive.

The *you* you have always been is not an easy thing to change. Your conditioning has created a set of beliefs and behaviors that define who you are. Admitting that you need a change is admitting that you are imperfect. For some this may be easy, but for most of us, this is one of the most difficult things to do. But it is possible. Changing how you react and how you interact can lead you to creating the life you want for yourself.

The first step is to become aware of who you are so that you can understand your initial reactions and natural behaviors. Then, you must be aware of others. Our actual behavior does not always have to reflect our natural behavior. Rather, your behavior is something that you can manage and manipulate in order to relate better to people around you. This may be no easy task, but it is possible.

In mastering this process you will learn to accept the characteristics and traits that you were given while learning how not to be governed by them. You have to clearly define your strengths so you can use them to your advantage. Then, understand the challenges you face so you know where to focus to improve your results and prevent roadblocks. Be ready to change whatever is necessary to make the biggest impact in establishing relationships. Make an effort to not be controlled by behaviors that produce negative responses from other people.

These are the 4 steps you can take to begin seeing a difference:

1. Identify opportunities for improvement.

Think about how you interact with others. Is there anything you think other people negatively react to? Write down any characteristics that have a significant impact on those you communicate with. Consider any actions or traits that cause others to put up walls. Think of things you might do that cause people to react negatively toward you, or that you feel limit your ability to get what you want. If you can only come up with one or two, try to ask close friends or a partner. Be sure to remain open to what they have to say.

Now, you have a list of your characteristics and behaviors that could and do offend others. It is essential, when attempting to improve relationship with others, to work on the things that seem to have the biggest impact first.

2. Understand that you will never completely change.

Now that you have a list of characteristics you want to work on, you can take steps toward making small changes. Train yourself to recognize when these behaviors become an issue and be purposeful in redefining how you react. By recognizing these opportunities for change, you will improve the way in which you build relationships with others. The key is to keep looking for opportunities and testing better ways to communicate.

Be aware, however, that many of the characteristics and behaviors you've outlined are deeply ingrained in who you are. Of course, these are not aspects of your personality that are easily changed, or even ones that you may want to change entirely. Instead, you will need to learn to adapt your traits and behaviors in accordance to the preferences of others. Some situations may call for you to be outspoken and assertive, while others may call for you to remain quiet. Being aware of your tendencies will help you adapt to your situation, and to recognize when it is and is not appropriate to act a certain way.

3. Recognize the traits of others.

Being able to read and understand people will be key to adapting to the needs of others. Begin by observing body language, hearing what they say, and listening for their tone. Be on the lookout for some key indicators, based on the DISC personality profiles. Do they prefer speaking up? Do they tend to speak quietly or slowly? Do they address conflict or shy away?

Then, categorize them based on the profiles. Do they match the description of a Decisive person? Or do they seem more Cautious? Would you consider them Interactive or Supportive? Based on the profiles, you can now determine how to best approach them and how they might prefer to be communicated with. You'll be more effective if you can adjust your behaviors and traits to fit with what they need, rather than what you prefer. I encourage you to start practicing on your close friends as you know their traits better. Once you recognize more obvious traits, do your best to mirror and match the behaviors they seem comfortable with, then move on to classifying those you don't know as well.

Profiles Revisited

Someone who is Decisive will be outgoing and task-oriented. Tell them the results you need, and let them figure out how to get it done. Don't try to force your will on them or micro-manage them. Provide brief instructions and guidelines and focus on the bottom line in a quick, direct way.

An Interactive person is outgoing and people-oriented. To work with them most effectively, approach them in a personable, relaxed, upbeat manner. Don't shower them with details or be too serious. Use humor, and let them know you like them and value them.

A person who fits in the Supportive profile is reserved and people-oriented. Approach them in a warm, but deliberate manner. Explain the step-by-step instructions for best getting things done. Let them know they can count on you and follow-up when you say you will. Try to avoid changing the process or tasks without a well-defined purpose.

Cautious people are reserved and task-oriented. To work well with them, provide the details they ask for. Be clear in your responses to their questions and confident in what you know, especially when discussing the task at hand. Be able to back up your ideas with facts.

4. Value the diverse personalities around you

As a leader who interacts with people on a regular basis, you must understand that no one is identical, and that not everyone will have the same style and preferences as you do. Your unique combination of traits and behaviors have gotten you where you are, but everyone around you will have achieved different goals and arrived on a different path.

Being able to recognize the value in all personality types will help you better interact with others. Valuing diversity does not mean that what you bring to the table is worth less, but rather that everyone at the table is worth the same. In interactions with others, it may help to comment on and compliment different styles, behaviors, and traits.

The easiest way to value the diversity around you is to be on the lookout for positive traits. Look for what makes others great and the characteristics in their personalities that allow them to excel. In recognizing these traits, you can support them and show how much you value their input. It may also help you to reflect on your own behavior and traits from the first step and then find where others might help fill in the gaps.

***

By first identifying your opportunities for improvement and understanding that change comes slowly, then observing those around you and profiling them, and finally finding value in the diversity of your co-workers, you can interact with others in a way that is mutually beneficial.

The best way to start this process is to take on the challenge head-first and not be afraid to try change. If you are willing to put forth the necessary effort, you will begin to see positive results. Develop the faith and discipline required for change so that you allow yourself to grow to your full potential. When you adapt your style to others, it will help you build a much stronger connection to them. They will respect your approach, trust you more, and think more highly of you. Nobody said this would be easy but it can be the most fulfilling part of growing through other people.

"To listen fully means to pay close attention to what is being said beneath the words. You listen not only to the 'music,' but to the essence of the person speaking. You listen not only for what someone knows, but for what he or she is.

Ears operate at the speed of sound, which is far slower than the speed of light the eyes take in. Generative listening is the art of developing deeper silences in yourself, so you can slow our mind's hearing to your ears' natural speed, and hear beneath the words to their meaning."

–Peter Senge

Chapter 7

Communication is Key

For much of my life, I have been in the Real Estate industry. First as a Real Estate agent, then as an owner, and now as a Real Estate business coach. Real Estate is a people business, so if you can master building relationships, there is a great chance you'll succeed.

Real Estate agents have to master their communication skills in order to acquire and maintain clients. The Real Estate business is one of the most sensitive to effective communication because agents work very closely with clients, helping them buy and sell homes. Communication is one of the main determining factors in whether or not a client is satisfied with their agent. If an agent doesn't communicate effectively or often enough, they are likely to lose business.

Yet Real Estate agents are not taught communication skills. Some agents don't even consider the effect bad communication has on their bottom line. When an agent loses a sale due to their inability to communicate, it can cost them thousands of dollars in lost business. On the other hand, an agent can easily triple their income by simply learning to communicate with people more effectively.

But it is not just the Real Estate business that requires great communication. I have yet to encounter a business for which effective communication is not a key success factor, and frankly it is one of the most important aspects to living a successful life in general. Yet, I believe we don't focus on it or educate ourselves about doing it better.

Although important, communication is about much more than simply choosing the right words. How you act and how you speak can significantly contribute to others' perceptions of you.

Verbal and Nonverbal Communication

In 1972, Albert Mehrabian wrote a book called *Nonverbal Communication* in which he discusses two research studies. He combined the statistical results of both studies and developed the 55/38/7 rule.[10]

The 55/38/7 rule is where 55% of communication is body language, 38% is the tone of your voice, and 7% are the actual words you say.

Although these numbers may not be entirely accurate for all people, it is clear that good communication involves more than *what* you say. *How* you say it and *how you act* while saying it are more than 90% of the message.

People with different personality styles often prefer different methods of communication. Some will prefer you to speak quietly and calmly, while others might appreciate humorous or more lively speech. In the same vein, some people may prefer direct eye contact, while others find that intimidating. Every person has their own preferences for communication, so it is important to ask how they wish you to communicate with them. In doing this, you will ensure that communication comes in a format they can relate to, which will increase the chance that they will hear what you are saying and respond positively.

Verbal communication, though, is becoming less and less common. We now rely more heavily on other forms of communication to exchange information or news. Written communication comes in many forms, including email, text messaging, and social media. In many ways, we almost completely depend on the written word more than the verbal.

Because 90% of the message is in the tone and body language with which it's delivered, the written word can be very difficult to communicate clearly. Often, your tone can be misinterpreted or your point misunderstood. As frequent electronic communicators, we have developed ways to overcome this to more easily communicate sincerity, honesty and truthfulness.

For example, it is easy to misuse CAPS or !!!!. They can often come across as aggressive or overly forceful while the user intends to convey excitement or happiness. This form of miscommunication can create a negative or opposite reaction than what you may have intended.

Successful communication comes from an ability to mix the ways we communicate to be most effective with the people around us. Communication is sort of like an orchestra with many moving parts that all come together to create a beautiful sound. An effective communicator knows how to put all the parts together to convey the most appropriate words, body language, and tone for the message they intend.

Communication can come in many different forms and can be challenging to improve when examined too broadly. Instead, let's take a closer look at some of the greatest challenges in communication: Not saying enough, not responding in good time, and not being clear enough.

When you don't say enough

People who do not communicate enough often find they experience a lack of communication from other people as well. It can be difficult to maintain effective communication if you are not saying enough to the other person, or the other person is not saying enough to you.

Consider this: You and your team have just been assigned a project by your boss. You realize after a meeting that you don't know the deadline and you're unsure of the format they want the report in. You get frustrated because your boss hasn't provided enough detail, but you don't want to bother him with follow up questions. You decide to just get working on the project without clarifying. The next week, your boss asks where the report is, and you tell him you don't have it ready because you assumed you had more time. When he looks at your draft, he asks why it's not in the format he wanted. Who is in the wrong here?

On one hand, your boss didn't provide enough information to you, but on the other hand you didn't ask for more details or clarification. The answer is that you both have a part to play in communication, and miscommunication can result both from someone not giving enough information, and from someone not asking for it. The problem could have been solved if either party (or both) had communicated *more*.

In order to overcome this challenge, make an effort to err on the more communicative side. When you worry about bothering your boss with too many questions, remember that it would be better to be clear ahead of time than to produce work that is incorrect.

Often, people are more concerned about *over*-communicating than not communicating enough. It is my experience, however, that people are either communicating with people enough or they are not, there is no such thing as over-communicating. If people are clear on your expectations or your message, you have communicated enough.

When you're not quick enough

The speed at which you respond to communication from others matters. From the perspective of the person who sent the message, your lack of response can indicate that you're indifferent to their needs or that they are unimportant to you. This person clearly has something to say to you *now*, so how quickly you respond helps them understand that you respect their time and their need for a response. So while the speed with which you respond may not matter to you, it definitely does to them.

For example, if someone sends you an email and you respond 3 days later, that would be considered slow communication. If someone sends you an email and you respond within a few minutes, that is quick communication. The same goes with voicemail messages or follow up tasks from a meeting.

Responding in a timely manner is not about having the answers right away, rather it's about acknowledging that you got the message and will respond with a good answer within a reasonable amount of time. You should make an effort to do this for every communication you get. This tells the other person you are listening and they are important to you.

If you think this is a waste of time, you are likely a one-way communicator. Recognize this as an area you may need to focus on and work to fill the gap. Often one-way communicators find only frustration for themselves and for the people they are trying to communicate with.

When you're not clear enough

Clear communication is not only about making yourself understood; it is about letting others know that you have heard them and ensuring you have answered all of their questions or concerns.

The key here is to stay on task and not get side-tracked by other things. If you have to communicate details or instructions, it is important that people leave the conversation understanding their tasks and your expectations. When those with whom you communicate leave conversations with unanswered questions or confusion about the details, you have not clearly communicated with them.

To overcome this concern, ensure that before you conclude a conversation or meeting, you ask if anyone has questions or if they need clarification. Try to follow up the next day as well to ensure there are no lingering questions or aspects that have become confusing.

If you find that you often need to completely reiterate what you've just said, you may have a larger problem with clarity. If you can, have a private discussion with someone you trust. Ask what you could be doing to improve.

The words that you use and the manner in which you use them has great power. You need to be selective with words so you are clear in your communication. The words you choose to emphasize are also important as that can often impact the message you are sending.

Clarity is power. That couldn't be more true when it comes to communicating with others. Remember, if you are indecisive in your communication, it will become more difficult to build trusting relationships. When you don't communicate well, people tend to shut down or shut you out. The clearer you are in your communication, the quicker people will begin to appreciate working with you.

Alternatively, if you find yourself in a situation where others are not communicating effectively, your best move will be to ask a lot of questions. When you need clarification, it will be better for you, and for the project as a whole, if you can ask questions to better understand the needs of the person communicating with you.

Communication is something that happens whether you know how to do it or not. Many people don't attribute their success to how well they communicate with others, but it can define how others see and respond to them. Most people think they are great communicators and that effective communication is easy. While this may be true for some, it is not the case for everyone, so you may still find yourself at the other end of miscommunication on a regular basis.

Reflect on some of your recent interactions. How well do you think you communicated? How well do you think others think you communicated? What was the outcome of your interaction? Have you had many experiences where miscommunication caused a problem?

Now that you've had a chance to think about it, do you still think you are a great communicator? If not, consider ways you could improve your communication. Reflect on how your tone of voice and body language might affect the way people perceive your message. Think about how often you ask questions and how often others ask questions of you.

Effective communication is one of the best ways to build trust and respect in any relationship. By ensuring you are saying enough, responding quickly, and being clear, you are taking steps toward ensuring you live up to your side of the deal. Then, asking questions to make sure you understand others allows you to take responsibility for both sides of the communication equation. Don't leave it up to others, they will appreciate it.

The Art of Listening

Communication is a two-way street, which means communicating is not just about talking or expressing your own feelings. The art of listening is more important than the act of talking.

You will learn and grow far more in your relationships if you master the listening process, rather than relying on talking and voicing all of your ideas and opinions at once. Don't get me wrong; it is important that you speak up when appropriate, but you must also learn to listen to, and take into consideration, the ideas and opinions of the people around you.

As ineffective communicators, we tend to only hear what we are saying and not what others say to us. Have you ever spoken to a person and been able to see that they were only thinking about what they would say next? These types of people tend to talk at you and ensure that their ideas get across, regardless of your thoughts and perspectives. The problem is that most people interpret this type of behavior as arrogant and insulting. People who have something to say but don't feel heard believe you don't care about them or their opinions. Listening is about joining in conversation with other people and solving problems *together*.

Good listening will help you gain fresh insights and ideas that will ultimately fuel your success. Most of us focus on learning how to present ideas more effectively, but using this skill alone will result in missed opportunities. The best communicators recognize that they cannot succeed without others and seek out information. They make sure to let people know their input is valuable and learn to become masters at truly listening to others.

When you show respect by listening to others, they will be more likely to reciprocate and continue to share ideas. This will foster growth in your relationship and increase the chance of them helping you achieve your ultimate success.

It can sometimes be difficult to hold back your ideas or opinions, but this will be the key to developing your skills as a listener. You need to learn to listen more than you speak. With practice and patience, you can control your urge to take control of a conversation and improve the quality and effectiveness of your relationships.

Good listeners seek to understand others. You can achieve this by first recognizing your strengths and your areas of challenge when it comes to communication. Then, you can learn to use this new skill to help you make better decisions and increase your effectiveness with people.

Relationships are Conversations

In her book *Fierce Conversations*, Susan Scott explains there is incredible power in each conversation we have. Every conversation either moves us towards or away from our business and life goals. She tells us that we are often hiding from our true feelings and we need to choose to be genuine and authentic in our conversations, share how we really feel, and work towards solutions rather than hiding behind ourselves and hoping something or someone else will change.[11]

Each conversation you have either lifts you up or brings you down, so you need to be aware of what effect you are creating in the conversations you have. Your life is a series of relationships; the success or failure of these relationships happens one conversation at a time.

Every conversation matters, so if you are not getting the results you want or building the relationships you need, consider re-evaluating how you interact with people. Personality profiling can help with this, as can self-assessment and self-reflection.

Universally, people long to be accepted and to be loved. In understanding this you can choose to have a better impact on the people around you through your conversations and relationships. By tapping into this basic human need, you can use it to your advantage by guiding your conversations toward positive outcomes. If you are authentic and genuine, others will recognize it and return the favor.

In order to have more effective and meaningful conversations, you must transform the way you speak to others by asking more questions and listening to their answers. If you are in the moment during each conversation you have, you can more easily listen to others and make them feel that what they say matters, that they are important, and that you're listening to them. In this way you can touch on a core human need.

Since you have little control over how others will react or respond, the most effective approach is for you to focus on your own actions. Be present, aware, genuine, authentic, truthful, and clear in your expectations. Although it would be nice for everyone to act this way, you may find that you're the only one. Do your best to maintain presence in conversations even when those around you don't seem to notice or don't respond immediately. Eventually, the respect you show to those around you will begin to shine.

Relationships are built one conversation at a time. Everything you say to other people either strengthens your relationship with them, or weakens it. I am not saying this so you feel pressure in every conversation, but rather so you remember that conversing this way empowers you to lift people up and connect with them in a unique way. Make this your natural way to communicate.

Each positive conversation you have with someone slowly builds their trust in, and appreciation for, you. When people begin to trust you, they start to believe in you, support you, and want to be part of your team. The alternative will be an uphill battle.

The best conversations are equal conversations, where people talk together and no one dominates or talks at the others. As Susan Scott says, "the conversation is the relationship,"[12] and if relationships are built one conversation at a time, then be sure to be purposeful in communicating clearly, compassionately, and appreciatively.

"I find the best way to love someone is not to change them, but instead, help them reveal the greatest version of themselves."

–Steve Maraboll

Chapter 8

Criticism Need Not Be Critical

Today we often find that criticism has become more socially acceptable than expressions of appreciation. I will admit, I don't understand at all, why that's the case. Being able to build others up, rather than tear them down, should be what is most acceptable.

We often consider criticism to be a series of negative statements that will likely cause anger and resentment. The question you must challenge yourself with, is how you can give criticism without hurting someone's feelings.

Although this can be difficult for most people, it is possible to change the language of criticism into positive statements meant to help others improve and progress. Most of us have a hard time *accepting* criticism without getting angry, hurt, or defensive and that is because, for the most part, people have a hard time *giving* feedback without seeming angry, hurtful, or offensive.

Changing the language of criticism is key to changing our attitudes about it. Rather than using the term criticism, I like to use "feedback". Not only does it sound better, but it helps me approach it from positive position. The goal is to be constructive, rather than destructive.

In order to be a good leader, you must learn how to give feedback gently so that the person receiving it can take it constructively. If your goal is to hurt, insult, or demean, you need to reconsider your objective, and consider how these comments may impact your relationship with that person.

In order to provide effective and constructive feedback, be sure to keep your emotions in check. If you feel strongly about what you are saying, take a step back and calm yourself down. Sometimes, especially in the heat of the moment, you may not be able to remove your emotions from the situation. As it is important that you always maintain control of these emotions, consider revisiting the topic at another time. If not, your message is likely to be misunderstood and the person receiving the feedback will probably get defensive.

It is important to know that feedback, when given correctly, can help all people involved grow as individuals and build up their relationship together. When you have a conversation about feedback, be sure to put yourself in their shoes and take into account their behavioral style. The ways in which people accept feedback can vary greatly.

While a Decisive person will just want it quick and to the point, you will find that a Supportive individual will need it sugar coated but with a clear explanation. To a Cautious person you will need to make sure you have the details and facts to back up what you are saying.

In any case, make an effort to put yourself in their shoes and give feedback in the format you think they will be most receptive to. A person who wants to build strong relationships must always think of the other person first, especially when having conversations like this.

Feedback should come in the form of open discussion about making changes, exploring new ideas, and considering opposing viewpoints. If your feedback is likely to hurt someone's feelings, or is intended to vent frustrations, you need to get your ego in check and understand there is no place for that in building good relationships with people.

5 Steps to Feedback

Giving and receiving feedback are key elements to positive change and improving relationships with others. It is often helpful to ask those around you for feedback. This helps you understand how others perceive you, and how you might align their views with your self-perception.

However, as a leader, it is also greatly important that you provide feedback to those around you. It can be necessary for effectiveness at work or even just a moment to show your appreciation for their effort.

The biggest problem with feedback comes when your comments are not positive, or when you are requesting changes be made. When you need to give constructive feedback, others tend to become defensive and distant. This is why learning to provide feedback effectively is essential for maintaining positive relationships, whether at work, at home, or among friends.

Providing effective feedback may sound complicated, but taking it one step at a time will help you get through the process. Here are the 5 steps to providing constructive feedback:

1. Schedule

Choose the right time to give feedback. There are instances where giving feedback immediately can effectively solve the problem or change behaviors quickly, and there are other cases where it would be more appropriate to wait and take time to consider how you should approach the issue.

Often, if the issue is very serious or if you feel strongly about the problem, you may need time to cool off. Remember that you never want to give feedback when you or the other person is angry, as that will often end in an argument, rather than a meaningful and effective conversation.

1	**SCHEDULE** Choose a time and place that works. Set aside this time to focus on your conversation.
2	**IDENTIFY** Write down for yourself, then tell which behaviours or attitudes are problematic.
3	**EXPLAIN** Tell why the actions are harmful to the overall success of the team. Be clear and straightforward.
4	**AGREE** Discuss and come to an agreement about a resolution. Work together to solve the issue.
5	**PLAN** Establish a plan to execute the solution. Set milestones and schedule check-ins.

5 Steps to Feedback

When possible, plan ahead for a private meeting where you can both sit down and focus on the issue at hand. Giving snide remarks or making off-handed comments at an inappropriate time will not lead to positive results.

2. Identify

Before you can give effective feedback, you will need to identify the issue or the behavior that needs to be addressed. Understand for yourself the issue in detail and consider possible external factors for their behavior.

Ensure that the discussion is specific to the situation or the behavior. Avoid going off on tangents, being distracted, or listing several problems at once.

Personal comments can often be interpreted as attacks or insults, and can ultimately damage your relationship. Making the conversation about the action and a suggested improvement, rather than about the person, will help you get your point across more effectively without triggering them to put up walls or become defensive.

For example, if you want someone to improve their typing skills, avoid saying things like 'You type too slow,' or 'You need to speed up your typing.' Instead, try 'I've noticed your typing speed is affecting your ability to meet deadlines. If you're looking to improve your typing, this class I took really helped.'

Be careful, as well, not to be vague in your comments. Making general comments like "you are rude to people," or "you are bad at your job," will not contribute to positive change. If you are more specific about how they are communicating with people or performing their job, you will be able to discuss potential improvements.

3. Explain

In order to be effective, you will need to clearly define how this issue or behavior has impacted relationships or the success of the team. Explain *how* the behavior negatively affects your relationship or success, and *why* a change is necessary.

If they are resistant, help them realize how a change could positively affect the outcome of your relationship and perhaps their relationships with others. Always come from a place of contribution and not criticism. Understand that when providing feedback, it is often hard to appear to be coming from a positive place so make sure you are sensitive and kind, ask many questions, and help guide solutions.

When providing your feedback, be sure to listen for their response and take into account what they are saying. There are always two sides to a story and often the truth lies somewhere in the middle.

You will need to be gentle and kind in your conversation. If you come across harshly, the session will surely end poorly.

4. Agree

In order to see positive results, you will have to come to a mutual agreement as to which behaviors and attitudes need adjustment. Here, be sure you are asking good questions and making an effort to be supportive and helpful while listening to their response. It's much easier to get people to buy into their own ideas than it is to get them to buy into yours.

Making suggestions is often perceived positively. It is more engaging and can promote creative problem solving, inviting the other person's input. This can make them feel as if they are a part of the solution rather than making them feel they are the problem.

While you may need to offer suggestions to get the ball rolling, you also need to be open to alternative views and encourage the recipient to create their own solution. Your goal is to affect change, and that process may be different for different types of people, so understanding their personality type can improve your results here.

5. Plan

Together, create a plan of action that focuses on the necessary steps to achieving your shared goal. Ensure that there is a mutual understanding of how the change will progress so you are on the same page with your expectations.

As part of your plan, schedule a time in the future to revisit this discussion. Review how the plan is progressing, and discuss the positive changes you've seen. Talk about how the change is improving results for you, the other person, and your collective goals.

***

Giving feedback, even when done for the right reasons, can often go astray. You'll need to know how to approach feedback sessions to improve your chances at a positive result. Most people assume the worst when approached with feedback. When they are asked to change something they do, or when they think you don't like something about them, people can be defensive and angry.

The good news is that you can change how you give criticism so it can be received as constructive feedback. If your feedback session does not go well and the conversation turns ugly, I would encourage you to end the meeting and re-visit the topic at a later time. Give the subject of your feedback time to settle their emotions and think about what you've brought up.

Providing feedback can be one of the greatest challenges when working with other people. Rather than taking on the challenge, most people just avoid or ignore it to prevent conflict. The truth is, though, if you avoid it for too long, problems can escalate and become much more emotionally charged or detrimental to your work than if you'd been proactive.

When you work on a team, or manage a group, do your best to be quick with feedback and remain in constant communication with your team about suggestions and improvements. Be careful, though, not to take this too far. Accept people as individuals, and only address behaviors that negatively affect your team's success, rather than personal challenges you may have with an individual. Don't forget to always give more praise than criticism, and to acknowledge accomplishments. This will go far in establishing a foundation for a strong relationship and will help you to be perceived as supportive and helpful, rather than critical and mean.

Admitting You Were Wrong

People in leadership positions can often confuse admitting a mistake with being weak. I experienced this once when on a leadership team. The company had made a mistake, so I sent out an email to our employees apologizing and correcting the problem. The owner of the company got very upset with me as she believed the email made us look weak. I realized at that moment that I was on the wrong leadership team, because to me, admitting mistakes demonstrates strong character and integrity.

After leaving the company, more than 70 other people who worked there chose to follow me to our new company. For the most part, their decision stemmed from poor leadership and our owner's inability to admit mistakes.

The truth of the matter is, you have to be willing to set aside your pride, your fears, and your insecurities to be an effective leader. You must earn, not demand, respect. In recognizing your mistakes, you show a high level of integrity. It takes a lot of strength and courage to say "I'm wrong and I'm sorry!" Admitting when you're wrong shows you are honest and humble, especially to someone who looks up to you. More often than not, the people around you will recognize this and appreciate you for it.

If you are somebody who blames others or makes excuses for your mistakes to save face, people will quickly avoid being around you as they will not want to be your next victim. People like this often struggle with relationship building and are incapable of building a strong foundation of trust.

Here are 4 tips to help you admit your mistakes:

1. Take Ownership

Own the problem and own the solution. Admit that it was you who made the mistake, and then provide an effective solution to the problem.

Commend other people who take ownership of their mistakes as well. Show them respect and support. In doing this, you will model the behavior you wish to see and create an environment that allows people to admit mistakes without being blamed. This builds trust and creativity.

2. Be Sincere

When you deliver an apology, mean it. People can easily see through insincerity, especially in apologies. Being sincere means speaking from your heart and being honest about what happened. Rather than making an excuse, try owning up to it.

3. Share What You Learned

Once you've made your mistake and taken ownership of it, let the people around you know that you've learned from it and that it won't happen again. By teaching people what you learned, you demonstrate that you care enough to prevent it from happening in the future. It shows the people around you that you reflect on your mistakes and make changes to prevent future errors.

4. Make Changes

Telling people about your plans for improvement is not enough. When you need to make a change, be sure to follow through. Take the necessary actions as quickly as possible so people feel they can rely on you. Talk is cheap and people want to see you do what you said you would do. You can choose to simply model your new behavior, or you can sit down and talk about the steps you have taken—your choice in this case is dependent on the situation. Either way, you will show your strength and integrity, and that you follow through on your commitments.

***

The best way to handle being wrong is to apologize and acknowledge it as soon as possible. Avoid making excuses or trying to justify what happened. Simply admit you were wrong or that somebody else was right and look for a resolution.

By admitting when you've made a mistake, you will gain the respect of those around you. It will enable others to become more comfortable with admitting failure, and develop a culture of learning from mistakes. Helping others recognize this as a great opportunity for growth will build up those around you and strengthen your relationships with them.

"You need to associate with people that inspire you, people that challenge you to rise higher, people that make you feel better. Don't waste your valuable time with people that are not adding to your growth. Your destiny is too important."

–Joel Osteen

Chapter 9

Final Thoughts

Throughout these pages we have examined how you can be more effective with the people in your life. The secret to success is in building relationships and adapting yourself to the needs of others. Communicating, providing feedback, and analyzing what others need will help you improve your relationships and create success for yourself.

All of these elements work together to create a life that inspires others to help you achieve your goals. It motivates others to work toward their own goals with your help. Becoming this person will require you to make changes in your life. You'll need to adjust how you react to people and situations, alter how you interact with others, and modify how you see yourself in relation to those around you.

Change is not easy. Especially when it's for the better, change can be incredibly difficult. However, in the end these changes are absolutely worth the results you'll see.

Changing your behavior for the better involves:

- Knowing what you can change and recognizing what is out of your control.

- Being creative and looking for opportunities that enable and encourage you to change.

- Remembering there are a number of right ways to do anything.

- Using your strengths to do the best you can and realizing there will be times you slip.

Recognize that growth and change are essential survival skills. In order to build better relationships with people, you will need to adapt and change throughout your life. Often, in times of growth, you will feel uncomfortable. Being uncomfortable is, well, uncomfortable. But, it's one of the most important things for you to embrace if you want to live a life of real meaning, purpose, and passion.

Get Comfortable Being Uncomfortable

Our journey through life is a series of changes—some major, some minor, some we don't even realize. One of the hardest things to do is create new habits or make active changes to our daily life. This is because people like to be comfortable and in being comfortable we accept the status quo.

Growth, however, is not about being comfortable. Growth requires you to be uncomfortable. Often, the times you feel most uncomfortable are the same times you will see exponential growth. That has definitely been my experience. One of my favorite sayings is that people need to get comfortable being uncomfortable if they want to grow.

Finding ways to accept discomfort as growth is an essential skill to creating lasting change in our lives and relationships. Putting yourself in uncomfortable places and positions does not come naturally, so you will have to constantly seek out opportunities to improve, and be uncomfortable.

Pleasure and pain are often webbed together and help you experience life to its fullest. On your journey to self-discovery you may find yourself riding a bit of an emotional roller coaster. You may feel insecure about your abilities and revert back to the way things were to avoid the discomfort of change. That's okay. It is important to understand that it's natural to feel a little out of sorts or frustrated when you are trying to make changes in your behavior and attitudes.

Growth takes time and doesn't happen overnight. Being able to do things that are easiest for you provides you comfort. Unfortunately, your comfort often comes at the expense of someone else's. Don't use this as an excuse to avoid change; rather, take it as an opportunity to make others' lives easier. Behavioral adjustments can happen rather quickly; it is a change in your habits that will take some time.

Adopt an Attitude of Gratitude

Providing positive feedback and acknowledging when someone does something that you appreciate can make all the difference to the way your relationship develops. People who make a conscious effort to be thankful and appreciative tend to feel happier and more at peace than others.

Adopting an attitude of gratitude towards people in your life can create an incredible change in your level of happiness. By simply applying this principle and adopting this attitude, you react to others more positively and can make an incredible difference in your effectiveness. It is often the small things that make the biggest differences. It's easy to forget what a kind word, a smile, or a thank you does to improve someone's day or make them happy. These small things are what make people appreciate you and make you feel appreciated.

Letting people know that you need them and recognizing their contributions are great ways to show how much other people mean to you. The investment in others will not cost you anything, but the return will amaze you. Praise your people as often as you can.

Pointing out strengths and recognizing their successes will help you build strong and trusting relationships. In times of disagreement or when providing feedback, others will remember these gestures and understand you are not there to cut them down or criticize.

People are often too quick to judge before they have earned the right or respect from others to do so. Seeing the good in people and recognizing their accomplishments earns us that right and encourages others to remain open to our feedback.

It is not just praise, though, that contributes to gratitude. Practicing forgiveness can prove to be the source of a great deal of happiness in your life. Compassion for others is one of the few things that will bring immediate and long-term satisfaction. In order to be genuine in adopting an attitude of gratitude, you have to learn to forgive and move on. Not only will you be happier, but others will be more willing to continue your relationship if they feel they will be forgiven for mistakes.

Your attitude of gratitude requires you to be purposeful in your engagement with people, acknowledge the successes of those around you, recognize the value others add to your life, and appreciate the people you interact with. If you focus on this, you can turn it into a daily habit and before you know it, it will become part of who you are. Give people a reason to appreciate you.

When it's Time to Just Move On

Building relationships with people takes more than just one person putting in all the effort. Yes, you should always take responsibility for the outcomes of your relationships, but there will be times when your effort proves futile. Successful relationships take the cooperation of everyone involved. You have to work together to build trust, respect, and comfort. When these things go unrequited, it may just be time to move on.

It is your responsibility to take charge of who you allow in your life and their level of influence on you. Everyone will have a different impact and no one can hold you back unless you allow them to. There are many people in this world that carry negative vibes. For those people, you can either become a positive influence for change, or they will not be willing to make an effort. If it turns out that someone in your life chooses the latter, you could find yourself in an unhealthy relationship with them. Avoid a situation like this whenever possible as one negative person can become poisonous to you and your team.

Who you surround yourself with matters a lot. Energy vampires will not only bring you down, but they will bring down the rest of the team as well. If you have them in your family, it's worth the effort to encourage them to make positive changes.

Some of the most significant problems stem from the attitudes and actions of the people around you. Here are some clues that signify a bad relationship:

1. Disrespect

If you feel that people are not being fair with you and are always pushing your emotional boundaries, you will constantly feel disrespected. There is a difference between someone who is pushing you to grow and someone who is pushing you down. Get comfortable being uncomfortable, but only when you believe it is for your own good or the good of others. Allowing the people in your life to constantly offend or insult you will not result in positive and uplifting relationships. In any relationship you should always feel supported through bad times as well as times of celebration.

2. Dishonesty and distrust

Relationships are built on trust and honesty. There is no way to have a healthy relationship if you don't trust each other. Trust starts with honesty, so if you want to build a solid foundation for relationships start by being honest with those around you.

Stephen Covey says, "Trust is the glue of life. It's the most essential ingredient in effective communication. It's the foundational principle that holds all relationships."[13] To communicate effectively in any relationship, you have to have a foundation of trust.

If you find yourself in a relationship with someone who lies to you or who acts shady, take a step back from that relationship and work on building the foundation of trust you'll need to move forward.

It is true that trust is earned, but respect your instincts. If you get a feeling that someone is untrustworthy, take that as a sign to be wary.

3. Mismatched values

Strong, long-term relationships are based on some common understandings and similarities. If your values don't match up, you are in for a difficult time. Your values and belief system are what you need to live authentically and improve your satisfaction in your relationships. This is what makes you feel good, so it is the standard you will hold others to as well. This isn't to say you can't be in relationships with people who belong to a different culture or religion. However, it is important that they have similar beliefs about how to treat people and build relationships, otherwise it will be difficult to establish a basis upon which you can grow together.

Your values and your belief system are based on your life experiences. They work in tandem with the boundaries you set and guidelines you follow in your life. This gauge defines what you think of as good or bad, right or wrong.

When those around you disagree with these values or act against what you think is right, you will often not be able to trust these people to support you. It is okay to end relationships when you feel your values are misaligned.

***

Determining which relationships are worthwhile and which ones are damaging requires significant reflection of how you feel when you are around them. Consider whether your feelings stem from who they are, or simply a few things they do that could be easily adjusted or ignored. In order to evaluate the relationships you're in, ask yourself these questions:

- What are my values?

- What are my boundaries?

- Do the people around me share my values?

- Can I trust this person?

- Do they respect me?

- Do I respect who they are and what they value?

- Do they respect who I am and my belief system?

As you grow and mature, you may find yourself on a path that takes you away from those you have surrounded yourself with. Just because you had a lot in common in high school does not mean you will continue to have those same things in common.

Life is about being happy, helping others, and being able to live purposefully. Your goal should be to always inspire others to live their own life in the most fulfilling way possible. Your job is to make yourself happy and then, unknowingly, you will find yourself making others happy as well.

If you do find yourself in a negative environment surrounded by negative people who have no respect for you and are always criticizing you, you need to make changes. Like I have said many times, you are only responsible for you and unfortunately, that means you may sometimes need to end relationships.

Healthy relationships are about mutual respect, understanding, and trust. In great relationships people take the time to really get to know each other and value each other. This could be at work, at home, or among your friends.

You can't make people be what you want them to be and you can't decide what is best for them. You can only choose for yourself. Your gut reaction should be to support, respect, and trust. Your first instinct should be to relate to people and help them grow. However, in order for this to happen, the people around you also need to be open and willing to build the relationship with you. If they're unwilling, it could be time to take a step back, or just move on.

An old Grandfather said to his grandson, who came to him with anger at a friend who had done him an injustice, "Let me tell you a story. A fight is going on inside me," he said to the boy.

"It is a terrible fight and it is between two wolves. One is evil - he is anger, envy, sorrow, regret, greed, arrogance, self-pity, guilt, resentment, inferiority, lies, false pride, superiority, and ego." He continued, "The other is good - he is joy, peace, love, hope, serenity, humility, kindness, benevolence, empathy, generosity, truth, compassion, and faith. The same fight is going on inside you - and inside every other person, too."

The grandson thought about it for a minute and then asked his grandfather, "Which wolf will win?"

The old Cherokee simply replied, "The one you feed."

Afterword

It has only been in the last few years that I've begun to understand the principles of managing behavior. I have seen a lot from managing people and I finally understand the value of building relationships.

I have learned the most about behavior by working among the world's most dangerous animals. My passion for the past 18 years has been wild animals and I have had the opportunity to work closely with them over the years. I have had to understand their natural behaviors and then be able to relate to them so that they would have the opportunity to understand me. My survival depended on me reading their nonverbal behaviors and responding to them based on who they were being at any given time.

As humans, we have the ability to verbally communicate, so many of us never look deeper than that. In learning to work so closely with these animals I had to start by learning to understand them at the core as *beings* in this world.

To learn to communicate with them, I had to understand them. In order for them to trust me, they had to know that I understood them. The principles and practices I have used in working next to these animals for so many years played an integral part in my ability to read and see other people as they are.

As you move forward in recognizing where you are and what your next steps will be in building strong relationships, I encourage you to stay open minded about this process. In *Winning with People*, John Maxwell shares many of the principles in this book. I found many of them very valuable in growing towards not only understanding myself but also in understanding others to build strong, healthy bonds with people.[14]

Building relationships with people is not simple. It involves many moving parts that fall into place over quite a long time. Relationships can be much like a beautiful orchestra: when everyone plays in time, the music is amazing. If one person plays out of sync, it no longer sounds like music. Remember there are many components to developing unbreakable bonds with people; each of them plays an important role. We need to take a look at ourselves from others' perspectives and be able to recognize which changes to make in order to develop the relationships we need.

Success in life starts with treating others as they deserve to be treated, communicating with others so that they are able to hear, and understanding others so that you will be understood. In this you will find peace, satisfaction, and acceptance.

Notes

1. John C. Maxwell, *Winning with People.* Nashville: Thomas Nelson, 2004.

2. Ibid.

3. According to the Merriam-Webster Dictionary.

4. Adapted from Maxwell,*Winning with People.*

5. Stephen R. Covey, *7 Habits of Highly Effective People: Powerful Lessons in Personal Change.* New York: Free Press, 2004.

6. Isabel Briggs Myers, *MBTI Manual: A Guide to the Development and Use of the Myers-Briggs Type Indicator.* Santa Clara, CA: Consulting Psychologists Press, 1998.

7. "Activity Vector Analysis." AVA, n.d. Web. <http://www.ava-assessment.com/>

8. Robert A. Rohm, "A Powerful Way to Understand People: An Introduction of the DISC Concept." P*ersonality Insights, Inc.,* 2010. Web.

9. William Moulton Marston, *Emotions of Normal People.* Abingdon, Oxon: Routledge, 1928.

10. Albert Mehrabian, *Nonverbal Communication.* New Brunswick, NJ: AldineTransaction, 1972.

11. Susan Scott, *Fierce Conversations: Achieving Success in Work and in Life, One Conversation at a Time.* New York: Berkley, 2004.

12. Ibid.

13. Covey, *7 Habits of Highly Effective People: Powerful Lessons in Personal Change.*

14. Maxwell, *Winning with People.*

About the Author

Jarrod Davis is a true entrepreneur at heart – always focused on growth and business development – as one of the top business coaches in North America.

As a coach, he is always focused on helping others build and grow financially secure businesses. His passion in leadership has always stretched well beyond himself in helping others create and build businesses worth owning.

Jarrod believes that everyone, no matter who or where they are, has the opportunity to succeed at a higher level. The path to success is found by leveraging relationships with others, understanding that everyone is different, and respecting everyone's differences. His dedication to supporting others is clear through his drive to help people create the life they design for themselves.

Jarrod was born in northern Canada, in a remote mining town where he trained as a competitive cross-country skier. He spent much of his life in the US and currently runs a non-profit in Florida. He, his wife, and his 2 boys split their time between Florida and Ontario.

Jarrod can be reached through his website,
adaptthebook.com